I FOUND MYSELF IN HEAVEN

A True Story of Death, Heaven and Finding Love, Identity and Purpose

Danielle Royce

LifeRich Publishing is a registered trademark of
The Reader's Digest Association, Inc.

LifeRich Publishing books may be ordered through booksellers or by contacting:

LifeRich Publishing
1663 Liberty Drive
Bloomington, IN 47403
www.liferichpublishing.com
844-686-9607

ISBN: 978-1-4897-3856-1 (sc)
ISBN: 978-1-4897-3858-5 (hc)
ISBN: 978-1-4897-3857-8 (e)

Library of Congress Control Number: 2021920000

Print information available on the last page.

LifeRich Publishing rev. date: 12/10/2021

DEDICATION

Dedicated to everyone who wonders if this book pertains to them. It Does! To my wonderful husband, Jim, who never left my side, and helped every step of the way. To my awesome children, Gabrielle, James, Jessie, Amanda, Michael, and grandchild, Conor, who were a tremendous loving support. To my mom, Jeanny. To every family member and friend that encouraged me and prayed for me through this. For all the people that came and prayed, believed, and agreed that I would live to fulfill my purpose. To Larry Keefauver who encouraged me and made me believe I could write a book and helped me develop my story. To Peter Lopez who pushed me to get it done. And most of all to the Lord who never gives up on me!

CONTENTS

PREFACE

"I DIED, AND I REMEMBERED IT!"

What is a preface? To tell you the truth, I think it is the part of the book where I tell you that I died, and I remember it! Not long after a back surgery, I had to return to the hospital due to an infection. While in the hospital, I died. My husband and daughter prayed for me. God heard their prayer, and I was sent back, and I remember all of it! Yes, I remember dying and I remember Heaven. It was through this experience that I received tremendous revelation that changed my life, and I know it can change yours. I travelled to Heaven, passing through death like a doorway, and came back. Dying and experiencing God in Heaven was a gift that showed me God's boundless love for me. Experiencing this love transformed and freed me from painful memories, health issues, depression, unhappiness, and a lack of identity. It opened my eyes to the truth of who I am and who God created me to be. My prayer is that through hearing my story, you will understand and experience God's love for you and have miraculous changes in your life, too!

MESSAGE TO THE READER

Dying is a big deal. Trauma changes you; however, it was not this traumatic experience that made the biggest impression on me. It was what I saw in heaven and experienced there that left me changed forever. I know you too can experience God's unconditional love and awesome power without going to heaven. It is my greatest hope that you can be touched by reading about my experience and experience God's powerful love in a whole new way. It is my prayer that you can find some additional perspective and see your life in a new light. If you will soak it in and ask God to reveal the revelations I experienced concerning my identity with God in your own life, I know that you will experience the joy of the Lord like never before. Therefore, I am dedicating this book to you. As you will find out in this book, God wrote you specifically into this book, so it is no accident you are reading it.

I will tell you that I gave this book my full attention the

way the Lord gave me His full undivided attention. I will share with you my revelations from heaven and how it transformed my life, my thinking, my total identity, and changed everything I thought I knew about my walk with God. It is my hope that the revelation of God's love for you will give you a supercharged revelation and purpose in your life.

I have only ever told my story to a few people at a time and it's usually in a private setting one on one. So, in this book, I will pretend it is just you and me sitting down for a long talk about how special God thinks each of us are. In the beginning, when I would meet new people, I would find out a little about them before I shared my story to make sure I was not overwhelming them with information they were not ready to hear. But because God told me to write this book and had in mind who should read it, in faith, I know God that because you are reading this, I will believe that God intended you to hear this, and you are ready for it.

I have grown since the beginning. I used to worry about what people thought. I now realize that it is only my job to plant the seed or water it, not to grow it. So, it is my intention to share the love of God and plant seeds of His love in your life and to be His hug to you on this day.

After you read this book, I will leave it in the Lord's hands to cause the growth that you need in your life. I have the faith that the seeds planted will bloom into all that God has made them to be. I truly hope this story will touch millions of people. However, if only you get my story and use it as a starting block to launch your hopes and dreams and this information helps you start living the life that you were meant to live, then everything I have been through in my life was for your benefit and I will count it as joy.

ONE
MY JOURNEY TO HEAVEN

I tossed and turned, and the sheets cut my skin. Fever wracked my body and the sounds in the room sounded ten times louder than they should. My husband had run himself ragged getting me things and giving me medicine. I had just had back surgery ten days earlier and he was doing everything to take care of me.

But it wasn't working. I was too sick. *This can't be normal,* I thought, *I must get help. Someone must help me.* I heard muffled voices in the other room talking.

I started yelling out my husband's name, "Jim, can anyone hear me! Please God, let them hear me. I cannot do this anymore. I cannot be this sick anymore. I can't take any more pain, no one deserves this much pain."

I thought, *I did this to myself. I got too fat. I worked too much. I did not take care of myself, and now I'm paying for it.*

I cried out to the Lord, "Please, God, help! Help me please! God, forgive me!"

Jim came into the room, "Danielle, are you okay? Do you need something?"

I replied, "Yes, I need help. I need to go to the hospital. The medicine is not working. I know I'm supposed to have faith, but I can't. I do not know how. I need help! Can you bring me to the hospital?"

I laid there feeling so helpless, like a burden. I remember saying to Jim, "I'm so sorry, I'm so sorry."

Jim looked at me and said, "There is nothing to be sorry for. It's my fault. I haven't prayed hard enough. I need to have faith when you cannot."

I looked at Jim, tearfully. I knew that both of us were feeling like we didn't understand how our faith could have failed. We were not understanding why, but both of us knew what needed to happen next.

Jim nodded his head and said, "Okay, we will go. It's okay,

maybe there is something they can do to stop the fever. I'll get one of the girls to watch Michael."

Michael is the youngest of our five children; he was only eight at the time.

I looked at Jim with tears in my eyes. He knew I was done and couldn't go on like this. I had reached the end of my rope.

I told him, "Call the girls, tell them how sick I am."

"Okay," Jim answered. "Don't worry, I will tell them."

I could not help feeling that this was going to be bad. My mother had always been the rock faith-wise.

I said, "Call my mom and tell her to pray! Tell everyone to pray!"

Jim rushed around to get all of us moving, telling me, "Okay, let's get you to the hospital, then I'll call everyone to pray."

Jim rushed me to the urgent care emergency room. We were there Thursday night and into Friday morning. Jim had called my surgeon and found out the hospitals were at capacity. We realized we couldn't get into a hospital where my surgeon practiced anytime soon. My surgeon instructed us to go to the local teaching hospital.

The ER doctor came into the room to find out what I was there for.

Jim quickly tried to lay out all the details. "My wife has been very sick with a high fever. She had back surgery, a laminectomy, ten days ago. We called the surgeon, and he changed her medication, but it didn't work."

The doctor replied, "Let's start by getting her into a room and taking care of her fever."

The nurse came in and began to take a more detailed account, got me triaged, and took blood. We waited for the results. Minutes turned into hours as I lay there tossing and turning on the hard metal hospital bed. I remember the thing that irritated me the most was the fever. It seemed like it would not quit. When the doctor finally returned to the room with the results, I was out of it.

I was in and out and everyone sounded like a Charlie Brown cartoon when he was in the classroom and the teacher was talking in a blur of words (womp, womp, womp womp, womp womp). The doctor spoke to my husband, and I tried to participate but couldn't understand her. My brain would not let me make sense of what she was saying.

She leaned in so I could hear her and spoke to me, "Mrs.

Royce, hello, I'm Doctor.... We have your blood results back and you have a very bad infection."

I answered back deliriously, "What?"

She tried explaining but I couldn't understand so she gave up on the details and settled on, "You are a very sick lady."

At this point, I was satisfied with that explanation. The idea was that now we would do something to cure it.

She said, "We are going to send you over to the closest larger hospital. You have a very bad infection. You need to get there sooner than later, so we are sending you in an ambulance to get you there faster."

The next thing I knew, I was being loaded into an ambulance to go to the teaching hospital in Galveston, Texas, 40 minutes away. Jim was upset because my doctor didn't practice there, but we knew the hospital, and we trusted they could handle it.

In the Ambulance

Once I was in the ambulance, I was very irritated and confused and began to complain to the attendant, "Can we turn off the sirens? They are SOOO loud!" The sounds around me seemed ten times louder and more intense than they should be, and time seemed to skip as I drifted in and out.

The ambulance attendant tried to calm me down and

responded, "The sirens help us get you there safer and faster. You won't have to hear them much longer."

Suddenly realizing that Jim was missing, I said to the attendant, "Where is my husband?!"

The ambulance attendant replied, "He is in his car following us to the hospital. He will be there at the same time as you, and you can see him at the hospital."

Hospital

I woke up in my second emergency room bed in the teaching hospital, and Jim was sitting next to me. Exhausted from the days of running back and forth taking care of me he laid his head on my bedside while we waited to find out what was going to happen next.

The doctor on call came into the room and said, "Mr. Royce, your wife has a very bad infection. We are putting her on stronger antibiotics, and if her fever goes down, she might be able to go home. For now, we need to admit her and wait on some blood work. We will get you into a room right away."

After waiting for a while, a nurse finally came into the room to announce, "Guess what?! Your room is ready, and we are going to bring you upstairs."

I felt relieved, and I jokingly replied, "That was fast. If it didn't cost so much, I would come to the emergency room in an ambulance all the time."

She turned with a look of perplexity on her face, an awkward pause ensued, as if she were unsure of what to say. I could tell she did not get my humor. I quickly jumped in and said sincerely, "Thank you!"

After arriving in the room, I looked over to Jim and said, "The room is nice. There is even a couch and a flat-screen TV. It is nice in here."

I knew Jim had been with me constantly running and getting me anything I needed at all hours of the day and night for at least a week. I wanted to give him a break, "It's like a hotel, Jim, go home or call one of the girls to relieve you."

Jim replied, "No, that's okay. Don't worry about me. I have called everyone to pray for you to get better. Try to get some sleep."

I slept most of that day. Saturday night, midnight came and went, and Sunday morning began.

I woke up in the bed, and Jim was asleep, slumped over on his side in a reclining chair. He had his good ear down to block out the noise.

This made me laugh a little to myself. Jim could sleep

through a freight train. He had one ear that he couldn't hear well out of so he would face that ear up and would put his good ear down to the pillow. That ear was his secret weapon to enjoy sound sleep. He has always had trouble in that one ear from a hunting trip when the muzzle of his rifle was inside his deer stand. When he took a shot, the resonating sound damaged his hearing in one ear.

I looked over and saw my oldest daughter, Gabrielle, asleep on a built-in couch in the back of the hospital room. *How sweet for her to be here*, I thought. I could see through the hospital window that it was dark outside. Realizing I was no longer feverish or in pain, I thought, *Wow, what did they give me? I feel great! Whatever it was, it worked! No more fever! No more pain!*

Then suddenly, I felt light. I felt like I was floating, and then I was floating above the bed. *Oh, wow! I must be dreaming.* I rose higher and higher until I was where the ceiling should be. I seemed to linger there for a moment, and I realized this was not like any dream I had ever experienced, this is different, it seemed to be taking longer and it was very detailed. I was experiencing every second.

For some reason, being on the ceiling seemed to be an indicator that I was not experiencing anything I had ever experienced before. This was not a dream! To coin a Wizard of Oz phrase, I was not in Kansas anymore. Then, my body began to pass through the ceiling, but I could still see my family below me sleeping in the room.

Then, in a moment, less than a blink of an eye, my focus was no longer looking down at my family. In that instant, it was as if that world did not exist. I was in a different place. The world behind me was gone. I was totally in the moment. Anything from before was wiped from my memory. I did not remember my life. At that moment, my current life was more like the remnants of a dream or a distant memory. The world in front of me was what was real.

There was white light all around me. It was so bright it was like standing in the middle of the sun, but brighter. It was like being underwater, enveloped in love, as if love were a tangible thing and you could swim in it. I had no pain.

I realized I was not alone. I was surrounded by the tangible presence of God, the presence of the Lord. I was getting the answer to questions that my brain did not have time to ask yet, all downloaded at one time. His presence was overwhelming love. It was all I felt. His love answered all the questions. I cannot explain how I could have questions that were being answered without the memory of the world behind me as a reference, but it was as if I knew everything at once.

In this moment, I knew that love filled me up. I could sense that God loved me. God's love was so pure and deliberate. He loves each one of us and knows every little detail of our lives; every hurt, and every happiness. He desires to be an intimate part of our lives and to hold our hearts and hands and guide us to the truth of His love. I was flooded with so much information all at once. I know that what we need to do is love more.

That is all my mind could hold onto. There is nothing more than love. I felt the love all around me like a big hug. I knew I was home and that the missing piece of me was in this place, and I was being filled. The details of my life seemed so far away from me now, like a faint memory. I did not desire to go back to the world.

The closest thing I can relate to this is remembering being a small child and holding onto my mother in the pool. The water was warm, and the sun was beaming down on us. There was a slight breeze that cooled my skin, but I could feel the heat from the water and the sun on my face. My eyes were closed tight and there was a bright indescribable color on the inside of my mind. My mother was twirling me around in the pool, and I was partially floating with my arms around her neck and my eyes closed. We were quiet, and it was the most nurturing moment. I felt seamless and my mind was numb to anything but that moment. This is how it felt in heaven, but a thousand times more. That is the only way I can describe it.

We did not talk about anything that was being said. It was being instantly downloaded into my mind. I just knew. However, now I realize I did not know everything. I did not connect that I had to die for me to be here. I did not remember my family or worry for them or myself. I only felt the tangible powerful presence of God. I was getting a download and was suddenly caught up to the truth and overwhelming love.

Then in the distance, about 20 feet away, I saw someone in front of me. It was a female person. She was heavenly. Her hair was long, wavy, and brown. I don't quite remember what she was wearing. It did not stand out and did not detract from her. She was enough to keep all of my attention. I began to focus on her eyes.

I moved closer and thought, "She is important; I need to get closer to her."

The moment I thought about it, I was there. I moved by the power of thought!

I looked into her eyes. I was taken aback because I recognized her eyes. They were my eyes!

"Was this me?" I asked myself, "Am I her?" As if it was a heavenly reflection of how I was purposed to be. This was real and what I had been on earth was somehow not true. This represented the glorified me, the one that the Creator made in his image. The one that shines through our earthly form when we walk in the Spirit with the Lord.

Knowing instantly that the answer was yes, I was so overwhelmed that I backed up to my original spot quickly. Then I reveled in the moment! I asked audibly to God, is this my new body, as if I knew exactly how things worked here. I was like a caterpillar seeing myself as a butterfly for the first time. I wholeheartedly wanted to be this new creature, and encompass all the beauty and glory that she embodied. I never knew what the words fullness of joy meant before I went to heaven. However, this was it, complete joy. The moment left nothing wanting. There are no words to describe how wonderful I felt. It was the most happiness I had ever experienced.

It is important to point out that I didn't know the person I was on earth. She was the remnant of something that I had just woken up from like a bad dream. I had none of the self-doubt, poor self-esteem, no remembrance of the anxious, depressed, overweight me, or the one who had been in so much pain. I was elated! All I knew was this was an awesome thing that was happening to me. I was jubilant. At that moment, I could not remember any experiences from earth. I was totally in the moment.

I did not have any realization of what had to happen for me to be there. I did not think for one moment that I had died. I did not think about my husband, my children, earth, or anything down here. I did not have a sense of the past. To think about the past would take away from the present. I only knew the present moments, overwhelming peace and love, and that I was truly the person I saw before me.

To remember the old me would take away from the moment. It would mean that I had to be in two places at the same time. I was in the present moment and moving forward. She was beautiful, strong, and complete. She was perfect. Now, I know that it was God's true version of me although, up until that moment, I had never known or even imagined this heavenly version of me. I just knew that this version of me was better, much better. This version of me was stronger, wiser, healthier, more attractive, original and authentic, full of heavenly purpose, a true masterpiece. I did not remember the me I had left behind; her illness, her weight, her aches, pains, her missing teeth, her past that forever haunted her, or even her present that was always incomplete.

All I knew at that moment was that moment. I knew that this was who I was, like a caterpillar turning into a butterfly, the best me, and I wanted to go and be complete. I wanted to be everything that God designed me to be. I was flooded with emotion, elated at the thought, and ready to move on.

While I was living my best moment, my awesome husband was back on earth experiencing something very different.

TWO
MEANWHILE ON EARTH, JIM'S STORY

In my distress I cried to the LORD, And He heard me. – Psalm 120:1 (NKJV)

It was a Saturday night when I went to sleep. I had been either in the urgent care ER, or in the hospital since Thursday with Danielle. Danielle had been in excruciating pain for months leading up to her surgery. I had done everything I could to help her. She had dealt with the recovery and pain and now the fever and infection. I felt anxious and tired, but mostly sleep deprived. She seemed to have finally settled down and seemed less restless although her fever persisted. They had finally gotten her into a private room. Gabrielle, my oldest daughter, had come to join me. The choices for sleep were a recliner or a built-in couch in the back of the room. I gave Gabrielle the couch and I took the chair that reclined. I thought "no bother" at this point, I can sleep anywhere. The resident doctors put Danielle on stronger antibiotics and pain medication to settle her down.

The head doctor would be in on Monday to see how she was progressing. I started to feel like the infection was not as serious as we had originally thought, because she was not placed on any monitoring equipment. I was concerned that we were in a teaching hospital, and the resident doctors were only a few weeks into a brand-new rotation. I was getting the impression that they would have preferred her to be treated by her own doctor and this whole thing followed under his care. I still felt relief that we were in a hospital environment and were not at home making phone calls.

I was sure that they would get a handle on it, and she could be transferred back under her doctor's care on Monday. I figured we would only be there through Monday and would be sent back to her doctor to deal with whatever this was. Regardless, right now she was resting and seemed to be getting better. I had been monitoring her the last couple of days as she tossed and turned and panicked because she was in so much pain. I was thankful to be somewhere she could receive better care.

I adjusted myself in my chair into the best position to use my old trick to cancel out noise. I put my good ear down. I usually slept with my good ear down and my deaf ear up. This allowed me to sleep through all kinds of noise. Danielle had always been a light sleeper, but I usually had to be shoved to be woken up.

I had an amusing thought cross my mind about our son Michael, as I settled in for the long night. When he was a baby, Danielle used to tease me because Michael would wake up for that 2 a.m. feeding. He could be a few feet away from me and be as loud as he wanted, and I could sleep through it. Danielle used to say it was my secret weapon for sleep. My ear problem came from a rifle muzzle being too far inside a hunting stand when I took a shot. I never heard the same way out of that ear again, but I benefited by having many restful nights.

I felt confident, like I could finally let down my guard and rest a little that night. I put my good ear down and settled in for the night. A strange thing happened a few hours later. I woke up oddly enough, because I thought I heard a sound. I looked at the clock. It was about 4 a.m. I looked over at Danielle. Her color was ghostly grey, and she was not moving. Danielle is an extremely light sleeper, so I reached out and brushed her arm. This always did the trick.

Danielle did not respond, so I got up, walked around the

bed, and said her name in a loud firm voice. She gurgled a little. I took a firmer grip, and I shook her and called out her name louder. She didn't respond. My heart pounded out of my chest as I realized she wasn't breathing! I hardly recognized my own voice as I choked out the words in a panicked voice to the nursing assistant coming into the room in order to check her blood pressure.

"She is not breathing!"

Meanwhile, a charge nurse decided to break up the monotony of the evening and take an unplanned stroll down the hallway in our direction. She happened to be a few feet away, when the nursing assistant turned to look down the hall and said in a startled voice, "Call a code!"

The nurse immediately ran into the room, popped a lever on the bed to flatten it, and called a code over the intercom system. She began CPR like she had been doing it every day all her life. Later, I found out the charge nurse that night had, in fact, never performed CPR on a live person before. She was incredibly responsive, and to watch her, I never would have known. People began pouring into the room.

Shocked, I looked around the room for something to do and began shoving furniture out of the way to make room for them. It was surreal, and my worst nightmare. Gabrielle got a rude awakening. She burst into tears and ran out into the hallway.

Jim's Prayer

As more people came into the room, I prayed a religious prayer, "Lord Jesus, I speak life into my wife's body!" My tone in my spirit was like I had heard on a TV, you know the scene where Jesus says in a loud booming voice, "Lazarus, come forth!" Only for me, nothing happened.

The room was chaotic and everyone there had something to do. Feeling that I would be in the way, I decided to get out of the way. I went into the hallway to check on Gabrielle.

I heard someone yell out, "Where is the crash cart?"

Every hair stood up on my body as the thought hit me that it was possible that they were serious. I wanted to yell, "What do you mean, where is the crash cart? This is a hospital!" My thoughts were interrupted when thankfully, someone came rushing by me with the crash cart.

Gabby got my attention because she was in the hallway crying and fervently praying out loud in tongues. I reached out and hugged her and prayed along with her. We could hear them in the room working. I heard the count, "1, 2, 3, Clear!" And then the sound of paddles emitting electricity, and I held my breath before I heard the dreaded words, "No pulse."

Minutes seemed like agonizing hours, and questions raced through my mind like a flash flood. I tried to rationalize to myself what was happening, grasping for details that made sense, asking myself questions like, "How long had it been since this had started?" I tried to remember if I had looked at the time on the clock when I first woke up. I remembered it was around 4 a.m. In my mind, I was trying to think about how many minutes it had been. It had to be at least 3 or 4 minutes. I had woken up, touched her, the CNA came in, and then the nurse. How long had she not been breathing before that? She was grey when I saw her. Then it took time to get the crash cart, 5 minutes maybe. We did not have much time left.

Suddenly, I had visions of going home and telling my eight-year-old son Michael that his mom was not coming home. Pain and panic gripped my heart. I thought of our marriage and how much I loved Danielle and our children with all my heart. Then the count started again, "1, 2, 3, Clear! No pulse." Our life flashed before my eyes… how she would no longer be with me to talk to, to laugh with, to spend time with, to live my life and grow old with, and how devastating this would be for our children. I had an overwhelming moment at the thought of being a single parent again and not having Danielle by my side.

Emotion welled up in my throat and tears welled up in my eyes. They were yelling out for someone saying, "Get a respiratory therapist up here!"

They couldn't get the intubation tube down her throat, and I heard them say they couldn't get a vein. The sound of a drill started as they drilled into the marrow of her leg to administer medications. Our future was looking bleak. It felt like those moments were going on forever. It got real! My heart dropped to the floor as the person I thought might be the respiratory therapist rushed past me into the room.

I got real with God and took a deep breath. With all my heart I said what I thought seemed to be a selfish prayer, but I was at the end of orchestrating prayers that might sound good. I said what I felt and did so with my whole heart, with all of the emotions, fears, and faith wrapped up in it.

In a shaky voice full of emotion, and tears in my eyes, I said, "Lord, please, please… I do not want to be a single father again; I do not want my children not to have their mother."

I hugged Gabby and gulped, and time stood still. A few moments later, a commotion was happening in the room, and

I heard a new voice in the room. The respiratory therapist, who had not yet gotten the tube down her throat, said in a shocked voice, "Hold on, she is talking."

I heard everyone talking and could sense the shock wave in the voices of the staff in the room. Everyone was shocked as Danielle simply woke up and was asking questions, and not in a sickly or confused way, but like she was in a regular conversation! They immediately started asking her questions, and she was answering them.

Overwhelmed with joy and sensing that we had just gotten an answer to a prayer, I said, "Praise God!"

The whole room seemed to move in unison as they wrapped up all the gear and began to bring her down to ICU. Gabrielle and I stood there in shock as they rolled her bed by.

Danielle was yelling at me and reaching her hand outside the bed and saying in an excited voice, "Jim, they are moving me, come with me!"

The nurse turned to me and said, "Go with your wife."

I said, "My daughter?"

She said, "I'll take care of her."

I crammed myself into the elevator with Danielle and she asked, "What is going on?"

I said, "You died."

She answered back, "I didn't die."

I said, "Yes, you did, you died."

She answered back with a question in her voice, "I died?"

She was rushed down for cat scans and more tests. It was then they discovered that she had septicemia and a huge abscess in her back next to her spine. We would also find out that she was in kidney failure. She was rushed into another surgery to clean out the abscess. The next few days were tense. She was put on heavy pain medication to deal with the pain she would be feeling. I immediately started reaching out to the family to tell them what was happening and to ask for their prayers.

Every time Danielle woke up for the next several days, she would ask me repeatedly to tell her what happened as if she were pondering it and trying to figure it out.

I have to say this was one of the most teachable moments in my life as I remembered those prayers in the heat of the moment. I realized that my first prayer was very religious in nature. I was treating God like He was a puppet on a string who I could pull on at will and with special magic words, get His attention. Now, I realized the difference between my first prayer and my second. The second prayer was real. At that point, it was not me modeling something I saw in church or on TV. It was my heart right there on the line, laid bare, just me and God.

I thanked God for the opportunity to have my wife back. I knew I was blessed. The Bible says that every man has an appointed time to die. I believe we were given an extension of time. Why? I believe it was to tell you this story and to tell you that it is time to stop playing church and get real with God and make Him real to you.

It is not this life we are building up treasure in, but the next. It is only to fulfill our purpose and love people and bring them to the heart of God.

> *But in my distress, I cried out to the LORD.*
> *yes, I prayed to my God for help.*
> *He heard me from His sanctuary;*
> *my cry to him reached his ears*
> (Psalm 18:6 NLT).

Gabrielle's Miracle Moment

In the hallway praying for me, my daughter Gabrielle had a miracle moment of her own. We were a blended family and Gabrielle was the oldest of our five children. She was always super quiet, responsible, and tough. Gabrielle had become a Christian when she was very young and had received the baptism of the Holy Spirit with the evidence of speaking in tongues. Although she had experienced the Holy Spirit in her life, she was not a religious person at all. Most of the time, it was hard to get her to even go to church. She had been to church but preferred most of the time to be a loner and attached herself to animals. Because she had been abused by her biological father, she kept to herself. She trusted animals more than people.

Gabrielle broke down now and then and let people in, but because of being sexually abused by her biological father when she was a child, she didn't let many people get close to her, especially men. Jim joined Gabrielle in the hallway and threw his arms around her in a big hug. Gabrielle was in the hall outside the room praying in tongues through her tears. Gabrielle crossed some boundaries that day she had never had to cross before. According to Jim, she was praying out loud in the hall. This was a bold move for a shy girl. She was enacting her faith like never before.

She had to depend on two fathers that day—her stepfather, Jim, and her heavenly Father. She had to accept a hug from her stepfather and agree with him in prayer. She also had to trust that the tongues she could not understand with her own ears would reach her heavenly Father's ears and convey her heartfelt prayer that I would not die.

I believe this moment put my daughter on the path to healing. Well, I am here, so God, in His heavenly nature, loved and listened to my daughter's and my husband's heartfelt prayers. I am not telling you that we must be broken for God to hear us. Please do not misunderstand me. I am telling you that faith means coming to the end of what you can fathom and fully convinced that you can trust God with the outcome because He knows the beginning from the end. He is a loving God who loves you more than you can think or imagine. Therefore, you can trust Him with all your circumstances, whatever their outcomes.

THREE
MEANWHILE IN HEAVEN

During the time Jim and Gabrielle were praying, I was seeing myself for the first time in heaven. I stood there - basking in the wonder of God's presence and seeing my true identity for the first time, getting downloaded with all that had been missing in my life, understanding God's deep love for me and the world and seeing myself for the first time. Information passed back and forth without a sound, sort of telepathically in complete thoughts and images. I believe that God heard Gabby and Jim's prayers and answered them by saying to me in an out loud voice, "You have a family." It is hard to describe, but his voice was resolute, and this simple sentence spoke volumes. So much power was wrapped up in simple words that mean so much more. Up until I heard those words from the Lord, I was totally content with moving on in heaven. I had no recollection of my family; only the moment I was in. It was only after He said those words that I remembered my family. It was as if God saying those words activated my memory of the world I had left behind.

"You have a Family" were the first audible words I heard from the Lord. They were spoken to activate my memory, yet they were also offering me a choice. The view in front of me changed. I saw a sort of portal opening with a purple haze around the outside of it. I could see down into the hospital room. All my memories came flooding back to me all at once. I could see the doctors and nurses rushing around the room. I could see my husband and daughter hugging in the hallway. It was sort of like looking down into an architect's diorama. I could even see the earth and had a sense of the chaos there. I felt burdened by all of it. I could feel God's heart break for the world.

Immediately, I knew my family, and I knew what had happened to me. I knew the beginning from the end. In a moment, it was perfectly clear. I was aware that I had died. I was aware of how my family would take my death. Like an old-time newsreel, pictures were rolling information by me like scenes from a movie, only it was my life. The information went on forever. I could see the people that were currently in my life and the ones that I would meet in the future. The visions of them popped up by the millions, faster than I could ever describe. It was discernible but instant at the same time.

Then, I saw people in the distance, possibly millions of them, in a line that went on forever. These were the ones I had not met yet, but I knew they were my purpose. I knew that everyone needed to know how much God loved them. I knew I had a choice. I could stay in heaven with its overwhelming peace and love, or I could go back and share God's overwhelming peace and love with others. I had a choice.

Not going back meant that my family and the long line of faceless people that I could have an influence on in the future would not hear what I was supposed to tell them. They desperately needed to know how much God loves them. They needed confirmation in their spirits that eternity was real. They needed to hear that God did not just love them generally, but that He had the capacity to love each one of them individually, and how each one of them has His full attention. They needed to be told, "You are God's precious child, and God values you. You are perfectly made in His image." They needed to know what I knew.

For the first time in heaven, I felt a rush of alarm. I felt burdened for my family and for all of you reading this book. God had shown me people on the earth waiting to hear about His love. He showed them to me in heaven lined up and waiting. I could sense His urgency and the importance God put on reaching them and letting them know that they are rescued, deeply loved, and that they too had a choice to make.

God wants to reveal His love to each one of us in a real way. We are his family. This was a revelation that people needed to hear. I sensed that part of my purpose was to tell people how much God loves them, and that He is interested in every detail of their lives. I felt God's heart breaking for each one of the people He was showing me.

I yelled out, "I have to go back!"

God answered, "If you go back, you are going to go through something."

Without hesitation or question, I said, "I will go through something."

Instantly, I was back in my body.

Waking Up to My New Reality

No sooner had those words finished coming out of my mouth, I was awake in the hospital room. I opened my eyes to see a bunch of people. Some of them were in motion, ready to do what they were going to do next. All in the room turned and stared at me with looks of surprise on their faces.

I was suddenly looking straight ahead at the resident doctor with a bright smile wearing a hijab. I remember her being a sweet female Muslim doctor who had been the resident assigned to me.

I looked to my left and there was a respiratory therapist I recognized because of the tube-like thing in his hand. He immediately said, in an exclamatory voice, "Wow! I guess I won't need this!"

I looked around for Jim and said, "I need to see my husband."

All I wanted to do at that moment was to tell Jim what I had just experienced. I did not feel sick or tired or in pain. I felt alert.

Someone said, "She is talking!"

Then they started drilling me with questions, "Do you know your name?"

I answered, "Yes, my name is Danielle Royce."

Then they asked if I knew where I was, what year it was, and who the president was. I got all those correct.

Then they asked if I knew what day it was and I answered, "No."

They asked, "Do you know what happened to you?"

I said, "I went somewhere."

They retorted back, "You died!"

I remember looking at my leg and asking, "When did you drill a hole in my leg and why?"

They told me, "Because your heart wasn't pumping. This is a procedure we need to do to get medicine into your body."

I remember thinking, "Well, I must have died. I would have felt that!"

They quickly wrapped up all my gear around the bed and started to move my bed into the hallway to the intensive care unit. I remember them rolling my bed passed Jim and Gabby in the hallway.

Excited to see them, I reached out for them, yelling, "Jim, they are taking me somewhere, come with me in the elevator."

I kept rolling it over in my mind, but the concept of death would not compute. I kept thinking, no, I went somewhere.

He turned to the nurse and said, "What about my daughter?"

The nurse said, "I will take care of her and I will let her know where you are."

Jim slipped in between the elevator wall and the bed as they brought me down to the intensive care unit to monitor me, do more tests, and find out what exactly was going on.

I asked a young male nurse if I could go to the bathroom.

He said, "Nope. You just died, your heart stopped, and you are not getting out of bed."

Obstinately, I said, "I need to go to the restroom!"

The guy said, "Just go in the bed, you probably already did. There is nothing to be embarrassed about."

I said sarcastically, "Really?!"

He said, "Mrs. Royce, just let it go."

I said, "Oh, come on, please!"

He started singing the Disney song from *Frozen*, "Let it go! Let it go!"

I busted out laughing and said, "Someone get a camera and put this guy on a video. He is hilarious."

The guy said, "Mrs. Royce, I am so glad that I can make you laugh."

Everyone was surprised I was in such a good mood and lively after what had just happened.

The thought kept running through my mind, "I died?!" I was really confused about that for the next few days. I knew for sure that I had been somewhere. If it was death, then death was like walking from one room to the next with no fuss and no muss. I could not accept the words, "you died." I guess I had always thought of death as a reckoning, a deadline (Ha! excuse the pun). Although I had met people who had said they had near-death experiences, I cannot call what happened to me a near-death experience. My body may have died, but my spirit was alive and went somewhere. What I experienced involved no pain or struggle. I just went to heaven. It did not compute that it was a physical death until afterward, talking about it and talking to my doctors and reading my own medical records. To me, it will always be that day I spent with God, seeing my identity for the first time and feeling God's love for the world.

After the test came back, they decided I needed to have additional surgery to remove a large abscess in my back.

I remember staring at the lights above my bed which had clouds pictures over them as they put me to sleep for the surgery. They had found a huge abscess in my back which had caused me to have something called septicemia. The abscess was a large pocket of infection next to my spine and they had to go back in and clean it out.

Septicemia, also known as sepsis, is a life-threatening complication that can happen when bacteria from another infection enters the blood and spreads throughout the body. It needs urgent hospital treatment, as it can quickly lead to tissue damage, organ failure, and death. In my case, the sepsis caused my heart to stop completely, which is called ventricular fibrillation. This frequently results in loss of consciousness and death because ventricular arrhythmias are more likely to interrupt the pumping of oxygen-rich blood to the brain and body. The heart is like a pump and mine had simply stopped pumping altogether. My doctor said that she looked up the chances of someone coming back from ventricular fibrillation in a hospital setting was 17 percent.

After that surgery, I had a sudden reaction to the antibiotics they were giving me, and it led to kidney failure. When the kidney specialist came in, he said that I seemed to be in high spirits for someone who had just died, had surgery, been sedated for several days, and had kidney failure. He told me he would put me on a special diet and see if my kidneys would come back.

Every day, they would run tests to see if my numbers were good or bad and every day I got better.

Then I had a drug reaction to penicillin and developed a full-body rash that they used a steroidal cream to help clear up, but it burned like fire. I still was fighting a low-grade fever and in pain. Suddenly, becoming allergic to penicillin limited the type of antibiotics that would work against my infection.

More complications came on the skin on my back where the staples had turned black and died (necrosed). The surgery area on my back was a mess. The doctor came in and asked if I wanted to do another surgery or have him simply cut away the dead skin and allow the wound to heal from the inside out. I wasn't sure the antibiotics were working, I had already died, had kidney failure, and two surgeries. I decided to wait it out and put a little more distance between me and this infection. That meant months in the hospital, healing from the inside out. Ultimately, I would have to have a third surgery, because it wouldn't heal.

Reconciling

I kept asking my husband what happened, trying to reconcile what he had to say with what I remembered. There were many times after that I would weigh what I was going through compared to the reception I was getting from the people I told what I remembered. I would tell them I remembered God and heaven. I thought it would be the most important thing people would want to know. It is funny, not everyone wanted to know. Many were even disappointed with my description of what I saw as it did not match up with their ideas of what heaven should be like.

The people who were most impacted were not church folks at all. Don't get me wrong, I had many Christian friends who were excited. Then again, I had others who did not believe me at all.

I had a friend come from church and ask me what I remembered about dying. I was sort of frustrated at the time with the types of questions many Christians asked me based on what they had read or heard from others. It seemed like my experience was so different from what others had experienced when they died. I did not like being different or standing out, so I told my friend all the things that did not happen. For example, I told her I didn't get the tour of heaven, I didn't see any dead relatives, there were no dark tunnels, and I didn't see Jesus. I was not in a garden with roses. Someone had even told me about someone who had died and gone to hell and was led out of there by an angel of light. I said I didn't see that either. (After that explanation, to this day, I think she thinks I went to hell.)

I eventually started to tell people my story, but only the parts I felt at the time they would accept. I generally said what stood out most was God's overwhelming love, seeing myself for the first time in heaven, and feeling an overwhelming burden for the world. To most of the people I talked to, I felt that my story was disappointing because it was not anything they had heard before. I got the feeling that what I believed happened to me and what they were hoping happened to me were not lining up.

It's funny because it didn't line up with me either. Feeling uncomfortable with the reactions I was getting, I told myself it was a dream in order not to have to reconcile with it. I could not make sense of one thing, and it stuck in the back of my mind. As much as I wanted to forget the idea of heaven, I could not understand how it was possible for me to be flat-lined and still remember everything that was going on in the hospital room and in the hallway with my family when technically I was not conscious in my physical form. Also, I could not deny the overwhelming internal love that I now had. I was changed from the inside out, and it wasn't just a new perspective, it was more. I felt as though I had seen the world through God's eyes for just a moment and understood for the first time how much he intensely loves each one of us. Little things were bugging me. For example, I remembered the purple haze I had seen in heaven and wondered what the significance was.

A few days later, I got confirmation about the purple haze. My hospital room seemed fine to me, but a few days later the nurse came in and said that they were moving me to a new room. I asked why and she said because there was a light over my bed that they used to induce seizures. It was not working, and they had to repair it. Within a few hours, they moved me down the hall to a new room and crazy enough it was purple! The bedspread was purple, the walls were purple, and the pictures had purple flowers. Everything had purple in it. I started to think that this was more than a coincidence. I had never been in or seen a purple hospital room before. They are usually blue or green. Well, it's not an earth-shaking confirmation, but it got my attention.

In the days that followed, I was having lots of reactions to medications, my wound was not healing correctly, and I was still suffering from all the rash from the antibiotics. I was miserable. The medication that they were using on me for the rash felt like I was being scalded. I was desperate to figure out something I could do to help my healing along so I called my husband's uncle who is a doctor and asked him what I should do to help with the rash and the kidney failure. He replied, "Imagine white light entering your body." This was not the answer I was looking for. I expected something medical, but the part about white light reminded me of the white light in Heaven. I suddenly felt silly realizing that the one person that could heal me was in Heaven, and that I had not prayed for myself. Jim and I immediately prayed, and I felt peace. In the moments after, the thought came to me to ask my friend Lauri Maulden for essentials oils that might help my situation. She had a Young Living business. We asked her to mix essential oils that might help with my rash and my kidneys. Jim came back with a diffuser and oils. It filled the air with the aroma of essential oils and then he put it on my rash as well. To everyone's surprise, the rash went away in one day.

I kept the diffuser going in the room because it made me feel less like I was in the hospital. The aroma from it would draw people into my room that normally wouldn't need to be there. They would ask questions about the diffuser, and ultimately our conversation would lead to why I was in the hospital.

I would answer, "Well, I died," which would open the conversation to talk about God and Heaven. I began to tell everyone who came into my room about my experience and how I came back overwhelmed with love for people. I wanted to talk to anybody about Jesus that I could. Heaven was an honorable mention because I couldn't understand it yet. I was still mulling over it in my mind. I still had lots of questions for God about why things played out like they did.

When I told my husband's cousin about my experience, she asked me a question that caused me to think about how I wanted to tell my story. She asked why I had not put it out there for people to find on the internet. I initially thought about making a video and calling it done. I thought I could get it out there on Facebook or YouTube and call it a day, but I knew all the lessons I brought back were important. I was still processing them. They were so big to me that I knew that I could not take the easy way out.

After some thought on the matter, I had to be honest with myself about my experience. I had a lot of reconciling to do and a lot of questions that I brought back with me. I struggled with them after I died and came back. It was only through God's grace and the Holy Spirit that I began a spiritual and physical transformation towards healing. After all, I had just been with my Creator. This was no small thing.

So, God did spiritual brain surgery on me! It took the renewing of my mind. I know that sounds religious, so I will say it in English. It took relearning how to think. It took dedication and giving my undivided attention to who God says I am. Through faith in what Jesus Christ did for me on the cross, that assures me that I am born again and am His beloved child. If God says you and I are amazing, and that we are made in His image, then we are. I needed to learn to own that fact and begin to put that truth into action. I had to figure out how to let go of the old me and embrace the new me that God revealed to me in heaven. I could no longer live like a candle in the wind of emotion that is constantly ruled by my actions and controlling me. I had to realize that even through trials, God could refine me and stabilize me.

> *My brethren, count it all joy when you fall into various trials, knowing that the testing of your faith produces patience. But let patience have its perfect work, that you may be perfect and complete,*

> *lacking nothing. If any of you lacks wisdom, let him ask of God, who gives to all liberally and without reproach, and it will be given to him. But let him ask in faith, with no doubting, for he who doubts is like a wave of the sea driven and tossed by the wind. For let not that man suppose that he will receive anything from the Lord; he is a double-minded man, unstable in all his ways* (James 1:2-8 NKJV).

I realized that although God was uniquely interested in my life and my journey, all of this was not just for me but to share with everyone I was to encounter. God is no respecter of persons. He loves us all equally and uniquely.

I had to determine what my purpose in life was according to God. All I knew was that it was different than before I died. Now that I had been through death, everything changed, and I found that I had a new God-given purpose. Walking that out was the only thing that could ever bring me true peace and happiness in my life once and for all.

Eye-opener

One of the shocks I had after coming back from heaven is that the words of the Bible jumped off the page and spoke to me. It was as if God himself were there reading them aloud to me, like a love letter meant specifically for me. I knew if I could help others to see this the same way that it would transform all our lives. Because the word of God IS a love letter that has a message specifically for you.

I know that if you catch a glimpse of how much you are loved, it will change your life. I hope that you will hear God's Word like He is speaking to you personally because He is.

FOUR
RSVP HEAVEN

Years ago, I met Don Piper, the author of the book, "90 Minutes in Heaven" when he came and spoke at our church. Several years earlier, Jim's mom Geneta, and I read his book. It got my attention. I had four teenagers at home and a toddler, and they were not exactly beating down the church doors with enthusiasm the way I thought they should. They came with me to hear him speak, and I bought half a dozen books. I don't know what I said, but I felt like I talked his ear off. I pulled him aside and thanked him for coming and that it was a chance to see my children in church.

I remembered Mr. Piper said that the people who greeted

him in heaven were all friends and family that had predeceased him in life. Each one of them had a special influence on him and encouraged him to follow Christ.

As I was walking out of the church that night, I said goodbye to Don Piper and asked what his inscription in my book, "I'll see you at the gate!" meant.

He said, "It means that whoever gets there first will meet the other one."

Then he said, "Danielle, I'll see you at the gate!" I knew in my heart we would.

After I died, the only person I knew of who had died and come back was Don Piper. My key takeaway, as I remembered our conversation, became to influence as many people as I could for Christ. My overall feeling was I needed to work on my R.S.V.P. list, whether I was meeting them or vice versa, everywhere, every day, with everyone I meet. I didn't want anyone facing a judgment that was only put in place for Satan and his demons when we have a God who loves us and has given us a choice.

Love Is What Matters

I realized we are all a personal evangelist for everyone we encounter. Therefore, right away in the hospital, I started conversations with everyone about heaven. I would have a good conversation with somebody, tell them my story, and we would talk about the Lord. I would tell them how much God loves them and how they were on His mind and in His heart. After my experience, every human being I came across seemed like a precious fleeting opportunity. I imagined the payoff for leading them to the Lord might one day be celebrated with a coming home party in heaven. I mentioned this to someone as I asked them to sign my journal with their information to keep in touch. They made the comment that this journal was going to be my RSVP list for a gate party in heaven. The idea stuck, and I started to lead with the question, "Do you want to come to a party? I'm planning one in Heaven someday." We would ultimately pray, and I would have people sign my book.

It was amazing how easy it was to lead people to God's love when I took religion out of it. I simply talked about a journey that we all must take and a decision we all must make as to whether to respond to heaven's invitation.

I would tell them that the only important thing is understanding that Jesus paid the price for our sins, that we are loved by God so much more than we can comprehend. He gave His Son Jesus to pay our debt of sin. Each one of us needs to live life with a purpose, love God with all our heart, soul, mind, and strength.

Then I would tell them, "I hope to meet you in heaven someday. So, let me take this moment to invite you to a party I am going to have there. God had you in mind and He showed you to me as I stood in heaven. Yes you, there are no coincidences. So, if you are coming, please pray and ask God to work in your life, ask Him to forgive you for your past mistakes, and take time to forgive others for what they have done to hurt you. Ask God to keep you strong in your resolve, to follow Him, and to guide you and help you make good decisions. Accept in faith that His Son, Jesus came to sacrifice Himself to give you back the choice for your eternal soul and eternity in paradise. Understand that God does not see what you see about you, He only sees you through the eyes of a loving Father. He wants you to give Him your life in whatever shape it is in, so He can give it back to you and give you hope in your life now and for eternity."

Then, I would have them sign my book as their R.S.V.P. for my gate party in heaven.

God's Love and Healing in the Hospital

In the six months I was in the hospital, I went through a lot of health issues. I was allergic to penicillin and several other drugs were not working to combat my infection. I had kidney failure and skin reactions to many of the medications. I kept wondering how I was going to reach people. How would people ever understand what I now understood if I was stuck in the hospital because my wound was not healing properly? I was wanting to tell the whole world about God's love and heaven, but my body was not ready to leave yet. So, I kept my focus on the love of God, not understanding that even in these most peculiar circumstances that I was going through, God was going to use me because I was willing.

I tried to settle in and not act like I was in a hospital. So, in faith I started dressing in my regular pajamas. I asked the Holy Spirit how I would get my story out to people and what I should tell them. I felt pressure to preach and for now, to start a blog that would leave the room I was in to reach people I could not reach in person.

The Holy Spirit answered me in prayer, saying, "You will sit by the deep well, and I will bring them to you."

So, all I needed to do was sit tight and wait for them to

come to me. The diffuser continued to be a draw for people. They would stop and inquire about the scents, and conversation would lead to why I was in the hospital.

From all appearances, it looked like I was just hanging out. I would tell them, I had back surgery and amazingly enough, I died. This would spark a conversation. Questions like: "Was there a tunnel? Did you see Saint Peter? Did you see your dead relatives?" and ones you probably have for me, too. I did not have all the answers, but I had the most important answer. I had one thing to say.

I told them, "Love! Everything there was filtered through love."

Everyone that came into my room got prayed for. Several stories come to mind from the hospital of salvation and prayer.

I remember I was in the last few weeks of my hospital stay, and I was believing God to get out soon. Many people came into my room during those months including physical therapists, doctors, nurses, wound care nurses, and people who would wander in from the hallway. I would start a conversation with every one of them.

The Lord would give me prayers and sometimes words for each and every one of them. I would usually pray with them about their situation and whatever they needed. At the end of the prayer, I would tell them about the purpose God had shown me when I was in heaven. It concerned the list of people I had not met yet that were very important to Him. I reminded them that God was thinking of them when I was in heaven. I told them they were a part of my story and that God's intention for me was to come back and speak specifically to them because He had heard their prayers, wanted to meet their needs, and send His love and hug back to them.

There was a mother who lost her children who I got to encourage and pray with. She had spent months sleeping in her car and desperate for prayer. I would have never known her had I not been seeking her.

A young nurse came in one day who I felt led to ask about her marriage, which was a question I never ask strangers. She immediately burst into tears because her husband had asked for a divorce that very morning.

There were people who came from the church to visit and had all sorts of questions.

Many people just needed confirmation that God was real, that heaven was a place, and they were on the right track.

I kept praying for everyone that came my way, even though sometimes I had in my mind that I might be off track.

Despite being overflowing with love, there was a period in the hospital where the antibiotics were not working for me. The doctors switched antibiotics and slow-dripped the new one, which caused pain eight hours that day. The question of why I was going through all of this floated around in the back of my mind.

However, I quickly learned that when I was ministering to people, any pain, doubts, or questions melted away about why this was happening to me. I knew that I was fulfilling the purpose God had for me. I knew that I was supposed to meet these people.

I must be honest though, I was anxious for the time that it would all be over, and I would be out of the hospital. I said, "Lord, if I am supposed to meet these people, send them faster and I'll pray with them and I'll talk to them. Then please just let me get out of here!"

However, there were more people God had for me to meet while I was there in that hospital room. One that stands out in a big way is a nurse named Faith that came into my room in the last week I was in the hospital. She was a nurse from Africa.

Oddly enough, I knew most of the nurses because I had been there for many months, but she had never been my nurse. The minute she came into the room, I felt overwhelmingly tired and fell asleep for what I thought was less than a minute and I had a dream about her.

I dreamed she had a family member that was in another country that was very sick and that she was thinking about going over there to take care of them. The Lord said to me, "Tell her to remember that I can get there faster, and I can heal them."

I woke up from the dream as she was walking over to add a bag to my IV pole.

I asked her, "What did you put in my IV?"

She said, "Nothing, I haven't touched you."

I said, "It's crazy. I just had a dream about you. I fell asleep like I was on a drug, and I dreamed about you."

She asked, "What did you dream?"

When I told her the dream, her face lit up with surprise and she said, "You must be a very spiritual woman."

I said, "I am."

She began to tell me the story of her father being a missionary in Africa and that her sister still lived there. She said that she and her sister had been Christians for a long time. Her sister had gotten ill and that she had taken this shift on this floor to make more time to prepare to go to Africa and take care of her sister.

She said, "I have been worried about it all day. It has been a long time since I have exercised my faith."

I told her God sent her this confirmation to remind her He pays attention to our needs. I prayed with her for her sister, and she was on her way.

Stories like this kept happening and I was just as surprised as everyone else. It had to do with me being willing to be used and open to the Holy Spirit's leading.

In the days that followed, there kept being hold-ups in my hospital discharge papers. I was scheduled to be discharged within the week, but the paperwork got held up for various reasons over that whole week. I was a little frustrated, but I thought this must be a sign that I was supposed to meet a few more people. I figured whoever it was God had for me to talk to had not made it to my floor yet, so I decided to go look for someone to talk to about the Lord.

This was going out of my comfort zone, so I sensed that I needed to plant a seed for my situation. You see, a seed must die first to grow. I had to die to face my fear of stepping outside my comfort zone and talking to strangers. So, I went downstairs to the hospital cafeteria. I had not been there before. I went with my IV pole in tow, which I imagine looked odd. I sat down and waited for a divine appointment, feeling that there had to be somebody that God wanted me to meet. I felt like this was the last person in the hospital I would pray with and then I could leave the hospital.

I didn't approach anybody. I just waited there for about 20 minutes and a man came up to me and asked me how to pay for his food at the cafeteria. Noting my I.V. pole, I made the joke that I had not been charged yet, but I was sure the bill was coming. This broke the ice, and I helped the man figure it out.

Then, I asked, "Why are you here?"

He answered, "I'm here with my wife. She's in the ICU."

I asked him what happened to his wife, and he said his wife had a stroke and that she also had diabetes. Her diabetes was out of control, and they said she might die. She was not breathing on her own and was on life support with a stroke and a tracheotomy.

I paused, feeling overwhelming hope, and smiled at the man as I said, "Well, I died."

At that point, I knew he was the man that I was supposed to talk to.

He looked shocked and asked, "You died?"

I said, "Yes. Can I talk to you more about your wife?"

He agreed and we sat and talked for a while about his beliefs in God and his family. I talked to him about what God had shown me in heaven and about the nature of God and the promises He made in the Bible for our welfare. I explained that there is an actual spiritual Kingdom of God and that Jesus had referred to this Kingdom when He said, "Our Father who art in heaven, hallowed be thy name, thy kingdom come, thy will be done on earth as it is in heaven." I explained that this section of the prayer was an important clue for us because it was important to bring the Kingdom of God to earth.

The big question, I told him, was how do we get it here to earth? I explained how as I sought to answer this question, the Lord revealed to me in His Word that loving God and knowing His Word (or how God thinks) were keys to the Kingdom of Heaven being activated in my life. Not only knowing the Word of God in general but knowing the specific promises of God that exist in the Bible that are specifically talking about us. I explained that the Kingdom of God is like a government. It has its own set of rules. Without knowing what those rules are and how they apply to you and me, and without knowing what our rights are in this kingdom, we get lost and we sometimes get run over. It is like going the wrong way on a one-way street because you did not see the sign.

I was blessed to have been given many tools. A lot of my visitors had come to the hospital with gifts. I received a lot of books that highlight the promises of God where the good news about what God says about us is pulled out into the subject matter.

I shared how it was good during my time there to go back through and read the promises of God. I was hungry for more of God and I had started to analyze the Bible. I saw where it said, "In the beginning, was the Word and the Word was with God, and the Word was God," and it occurred to me that if I was to know who God was, I needed to do what His Word said to do. I discovered God's Word reveals His personality. His intentions and plans for you and me are all wrapped up in this one book.

I explained to the man that he only had to read the New Testament to understand that it was God's intention to heal his wife.

"Everything you read about the life of Jesus is how He went around healing folks. I believe that if the Kingdom of Heaven is at hand the way Jesus said it was in the Lord's prayer, then according to the promises of the Bible, your wife has a legal right to healing."

God reminded me about how in Luke chapter 13 there was a woman who waited eighteen years for her healing. Jesus said, "Shouldn't she have a right to be free?" We have rights in the Kingdom of Heaven! I told the man that the Lord cannot lie. His word cannot lie and once spoken it is sent on a mission and cannot return void or without results. Our tongue is a two-edged sword. It is an offensive weapon, and we have to speak out loud, the promises of God concerning our lives and especially his wife's situation. It would go do the work it was sent to do.

I explained that speaking the words out loud was important. Speaking the promises of God over her situation out loud was not simply a protocol or a religious act but was a declaration of his faith and that he knew God loved his wife and cared about what happened to her. Speaking His promises out loud builds belief in us and them and allows God to work in our situation, on our behalf. The Bible says that faith comes by hearing and hearing by the Word of God.

I explained how we are three-part beings; we have a spirit man, a soul, and a physical body. We are either led by our earthly mind, or we allow the Holy Spirit to lead. Our body needs to **hear** the Word of God come out of our mouths. The Word of God has miracle-working power and if we are to have faith for a miracle, then we must exercise our faith. We have a faith bank account. God says that each one of us is given the measure of faith. Sometimes, we need to make a deposit in that bank account by telling our body what it needs to hear.

I instructed the man to fight for his wife. We went to her hospital room in the Intensive Care Unit. I had to get permission to go in as a patient, but I had favor and they let me go in. At this point, the woman was on a respirator. The nurse came in while I was there and checked her sugar, it was over 260. She was not breathing on her own. Everything I saw with my eyes said she wasn't going to make it, but what I could see did not matter.

What mattered was what the Word of God said about her. Which scripture were we standing on and what did we believe? Were we going to let God work on her situation? What were we saying about her situation that agreed with the Word of God?

I gave the man my God's Promises book, and said, "You speak the healing scriptures over your wife every day believing that God wants to do for you what you are hoping for."

Then, I told the man I would be back in two weeks to check on him. I knew in my spirit that my paperwork would go through, that I was getting out of the hospital any day. I made a mental note in my mind that two weeks from today, I would come back and check on this man and see that his wife was healed.

Those last weeks in the hospital were powerful ones. I prayed the Word of God over my situation and hung a sign on the wall in my room. It said, "I shall live and not die and proclaim the works of the Lord." I read in the Bible that faith without works is dead, so I began to book myself for commitments literally without knowing the actual date I would leave. I booked a real estate course. I booked a flight to Seattle to start a new Christian business. I signed up for a women's conference and everything else that I wanted to do outside of the hospital. I exercised my faith to believe that I was leaving that hospital healed once and for all.

Released

Finally, the word came, I was being released from the hospital. I was at home, but I still had the pain, I still had symptoms, and I was still very tired and very weak. I was on wound care and had a nurse coming into my home to help take care of me. I did not stop looking for opportunities to share, and I saw the nurse coming as an opportunity to share the love of Jesus. I said this too shall pass but that lingering question of *Why did I have to go through this?* kept bothering me. Why am I still sick?

I did not forget the man and his wife from the hospital. My two weeks came and went quickly. I went back to the hospital for a return check-up. When I went back, I looked for the man from the ICU. I went to the ICU to inquire about the man and his wife and ran into several other people that I had prayed for who worked in the hospital. They gave me follow-ups on how their situation was going. Each one was like a divine appointment. I got to pray with them in the lobby.

I found out that the man and his wife had moved to a room in the hospital. I went to the room and saw the woman sitting on the side of the bed signing papers. She had no respirator and they had removed her tracheotomy. She had no signs of a stroke, her sugar was fine, and she was not even going to rehab. Glory to Jesus! She was going home healed and fully recovered. The man was excited to see me and said that he had prayed over his wife as I had told him. I was excited to see him. It was a quick meeting and I told him to keep applying God's Word to all the situations that come up.

> *Confess your trespasses to one another, and pray for one another, that you may be healed. The effective, fervent prayer of a righteous man avails much* (James 5:16 NKJV).

> *The Spirit of the Lord is upon Me, because He has anointed Me to preach the gospel to the poor; He has sent Me to heal the brokenhearted, to proclaim liberty to the captives and recovery of sight to the blind, to set at liberty those who are oppressed* (Luke 4:18 NKJV).

> *Behold, I will bring it health and healing; I will heal them and reveal to them the abundance of peace and truth* (Jeremiah 33:6 NKJV).

I realized we are all personal evangelists for everyone we encounter. Therefore, I started conversations about heaven with everyone who entered my hospital room. I experienced the revelation that my Jesus lives and how He feels about me. I knew that if I could find a way to get you in touch with how much he loves you that it would change your perception and reality forever.

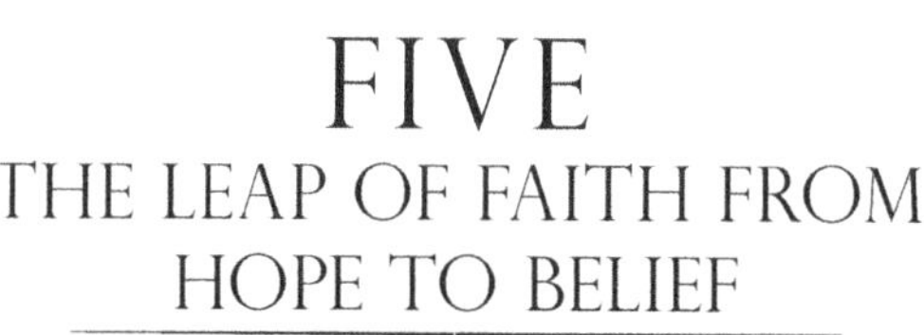

FIVE
THE LEAP OF FAITH FROM HOPE TO BELIEF

I came back changed from the inside and had a new beginning with God. I got a new appetite for reading the Bible. I had read the Bible through once at school and heard scriptures read to me at church. But now, reading the bible was different. The Bible to me had always been a set of rules and instructions. It was like having the author read you the book personally. I could just feel God's fatherly love guiding me through the words, teaching me their meaning and their true value and intent. The words seemed to jump off the page.

I would ask God a question and He would not only drop the answer down in my brain like a gumball machine. Eventually the thoughts that had been conveyed in my spirit, then would be confirmed in the word of God.

The word of God was like a love letter. I knew it was not just for me but for the human race. I knew from my experience that he loved me fully, uniquely, and personally. In other words, he loves us all and cares about all the minute details of your life. In heaven, God showed me all the people, people he cared about.

He let me know that I would have the opportunity to meet them and why revealing His love was so important. I sensed in Heaven that He wanted you to know how much He loves you personally and how much he wants to be real in your life. So, it is a love letter to you, too!

I hope that reading this book gets your attention. God loves everyone in the world, and it is our basic purpose to reveal that fact to the world in our everyday walk and in all that we do.

There is a key lesson I learned while I was still in the hospital. Although I was out of the intensive care unit, I was still in a battle for my life. I could not wrap my mind around why I was not healing faster and walking out of the hospital. I continued to have infections and medications were failing. I kept hearing in my mind the words the Lord had said in heaven. You will have to go through something. Was this the something I was having to go through? I thought: why did I have to go through something? I had more to learn about healing and through this journey with God. The upside was for the first time in my life, I had time to focus on God. I was in the hospital with nothing to do but pray and search and ask God for the answers to all my questions about heaven. On some level I knew that this going through something had something to do with my core beliefs.

> *Surely, he took up our pain and bore our suffering, yet we considered him punished by God, stricken by him, and afflicted. But he was pierced for our transgressions, he was crushed for our iniquities; the punishment that brought us peace was on him, and by his wounds we are healed* (Isaiah 53:4-5).
>
> *'But I will restore you to health and heal your wounds,' declares the LORD* (Jeremiah 30:17).

Every person I met in the hospital was an opportunity to share the love I had experienced in heaven. I was praying with folks and reading my Bible, but something in my faith was missing. I began to realize that even though I wanted to be at home, that I was meeting people that I would have never met otherwise. The people I was meeting were some of the many people that I believe God showed me in heaven, the people that God wanted to reach. I changed my attitude from one of anxiety and fear to one of thankfulness for every moment I was given. I prayed, "Lord, thank you, for this season, I might never have met these people if I were not here in this hospital for four months." I kept believing that it was only for a season, putting my trust in God that he knew my prayer. Nevertheless, I still had a nagging question. **Why had God said I had to go through something**? I knew God was a loving God, so I knew I was going to get the answer eventually.

Everything Is Small Next to Eternity

Everyone dies, and their spirit moves on. It's only a question when it will happen and where they will end up after the fact. I hit a low point in the hospital when the antibiotics stopped being effective and I started to have side effects from them like losing skin on my hands and feet and having the symptoms of C.diff. Clostridium difficile (C. difficile or C. diff) is a specific kind of bacterial infection that causes mild to life-threatening forms of diarrhea and colitis. The infection is often called Clostridium difficile-associated disease (or "CDAD") or Clostridium difficile infection.[1]

They had me do a test to determine whether I had it or not, but the hospital staff went immediately on alert. Since I had the potential to be highly contagious and I had all the symptoms, I was no longer allowed to leave the room or go to rehab. Everyone that came into the room had to wear gloves and a mask. I found out that this condition could be fatal to me. Feeling sick and tired, I got depressed and cried all day, asking God why I had gone through so much to end up here in another life-threatening situation. Antibiotics were not working, and they had to change mine to one that had to be slowly dripped and caused side effects like: muscle pain all day long and losing the skin on my feet and hands. I felt as though I were falling apart.

I panicked thinking that I was going to die and told a nurse, "I would like to make a will. Can somebody assist me?" I felt like an unfinished symphony, I had not really told my children my whole experience. I wanted to pass on what God

---

[1] c-difficile-treatment.com/what-is-c-diff#:~:text=Clostridium%20difficile%20%28C.%20difficile%2C%20or%20C.%20diff%29%20is,difficile-associated%20disease%20%28or%20%E2%80%9CCDAD%E2%80%9D%29%20or%20Clostridium

had revealed to me to my family. Thinking that I might never get the chance to pass on the love and lessons I had learned, I used my phone and made what I thought was going to be the last piece of wisdom I could pass on to my children and my husband Jim.

Summary of the Video

Do not miss out on the love that God has for you. I experienced the overwhelming love from the Lord in heaven. This love was so real and tangible. The love that God has for each one of you runs so deep and he wants you to experience and understand that love. It doesn't matter what you've done wrong or right, he is a God of unconditional love and forgiveness. When we make the wrong decisions there are consequences, but they have nothing to do with God's love for you. God wants to shield you from the consequences and missteps by being your guide through your life, helping you to fulfill your purpose and destiny. You have a purpose! Do not negate your purpose or forget what God created you for and what you're here to do on this earth. Do not sell yourself cheap for forgetting your dreams that the Lord God himself has placed in your heart. If God gave it to you, he will equip you to accomplish it. Some of you are so hard on yourselves, that you get lost. Do not work so hard or get so busy or distracted that you forget that you need to make time to stop and smell the roses and enjoy life. In the end you have all eternity ahead of you and good news, heaven is a real place, but you must choose it. The world is waiting for you to fulfill your God given purpose. There is no substitute for you. This life is short, and we are not home yet. Do not forget that the only thing you can take with you out of this world is the love you gave and the love you received. The only treasures you can store up are the souls you reach for heaven. Do not forget that God has a plan laid out specifically for you and God is on your side. Remember to filter everything through love and do not get burdened down with distractions, which are so common and rob us of precious moments. When you feel out of place because you stand for righteousness, remember you are not meant to fit in. Earth is your temporary home. Remember that your relationship with God is everything and that this life is only a millisecond compared to eternity. Time is precious. Focus everything you have now on showing the love of Christ to the people God has placed in your life. You will want your friends and family in heaven with you, so do not be afraid to share with them how much God loves them. Remember that I did not remember you in heaven because I believe that the ones you can know in heaven are the ones that loved the Lord and got there before you or the ones you influence for heaven, and because of your witness, you essentially take them with you. If you want your family there with you, you must tell them that they need to make a choice to dedicate their lives to the Lord, through believing in his son Jesus Christ. It is a daily walk, and they must dedicate their lives daily, not just on Sunday. Please avoid sin. It will kill you and destroy your life. Do not waste time on unforgiveness or strife. Do not let worry rob you of your peace and happiness. They are a waste of time and will rob you of what you were put here to do. Do not get comfortable, this is not your home. Remember I love you for eternity. God and Jesus are real so cling to the Word of God like it is your life's breath. It is my most sincere prayer that you know how much I love you and that you know you are in my heart, and it is my desire to see you again someday. It is my biggest hope that you will know how much God loves you and that I love you, and it is my highest hope that you live your whole lives for the Lord, and that we meet again.

Making this video was a pivotal moment for me. I realized I had many choices about how I would live for God. I was not sure what that plan path was, but I knew it was different from the one I had been on. What I did or had done in my life up until the day I died had forever changed because I had experienced God's love and saw my identity through heaven's eyes. I know that some of you have a sneaking suspicion that you are not living your best life. You are not using your gifts and talents. Is it possible that God has blessed you with a dream or talent and He has something else for you to do? Perhaps some of you are riding the waves of life using every moment as an opportunity. Some of you are wanderers and do not know what God has for you to do. Pray and wait on the Lord, stay close and in time he will reveal it to you.

I thought what I could do or accomplish was the key ingredient to God's plan. The truth was God is the key ingredient, there must be more of him telling you what the plan is, step by step. Remember God is a loving father, who wants to see you happy and successful.

> *Trust in the Lord with all thine heart: and lean not unto thine own understanding. In all thy ways acknowledge him, and he will direct thy paths* (Proverbs 3:5,6, KJV).

> *For I know the thoughts that I think toward you, saith the Lord, thoughts of peace, and not of evil, to give you an expected end* (Jeremiah 29:11 KJV).

God is not a clockmaker, he did not make you to just live and die, he made you to live and evolve from a caterpillar to a butterfly. He wants you to be happy, feel loved, know him, and through him live out your purpose.

When are you going to believe me?

Once I did the video, I prayed and asked Him, "Okay, Lord, I've told my family what they need to know. Is this the final thing I will have to say?"

The Lord answered in my spirit, ***"When are you going to believe Me?"***

Surprised, I said to the Lord, "Of course, I believe you, Lord. I was there! I went to heaven! I've prayed with all these people. Of course, I believe you!"

The Lord asked again, **"When are you going to believe Me?"**

Then as if the Lord flipped a switch, a light bulb went on in my head and I realized I needed to answer this question for myself before I could truthfully answer God.

When was I going to believe Him?
When was I going to believe that I deserved to be healed?

When was I going to believe that I did not have to live with this infection?
When was I going to start expecting my healing?
When was I going to believe that pain did have to be a part of my life?

God did have a plan to prosper me! However, he gave me free will so He could not overcome my own disbelief about my situation. He was having to do spiritual surgery on my spirit and work from the inside out. It was time I submitted to his spiritual surgery.

At that moment I stepped out in faith, and I immediately pushed the ringer for the nurse and asked the physician to do the "c. diff" test again. I did not have one more symptom from that moment forward. One moment I was dying and the next I was scheduled to be discharged from the hospital. This was a valuable lesson in faith for me.

So Many Questions Still

When people asked me what heaven looked like, I answered, "**Love**." When they asked me what God looked like, I answered, **"Light, Revelation, Understanding, Home."** Although I didn't feel like I had all the answers, I answered with the help of the Holy Spirit.

However, when I was alone, there were times I struggled with an identity crisis. I had so many questions that I could not find answers to. On one hand, it was a miracle that I had come back from dying and I remembered it. It was a gift of a different perspective of God's love for me. I knew that in my current state, I had work to do on me, here on earth. Up until I died, I was depressed, overweight, anxious, and addicted to approval. I was running from a lot of pain, sadness, and memories that the devil loved to parade in front of me. I was afraid that I would sink back into my old state of being, that I would forget all the lessons I had learned. I mourned heaven and all that it represented. I think for a season I was homesick for heaven and deep inside I was angry at God for showing me the possibilities, for showing me the woman that I felt I could never be. I was torn between the woman God showed me in heaven, and the woman I saw looking back at me in the mirror. The woman in heaven was the heavenly reality of all God's intetentions for me. She was how God had intended me to be before the enemy had stripped me of my Godly image and my true identity in Christ. I would share God's love and hope with people but somewhere deep inside me I would doubt and ask God: why would you show me a woman I could never become? When I saw myself in heaven, I saw the physical being but, had a second sense of all that she was internally too. I felt like a shadowy reflection of something far greater than I ever thought I could be. I knew that God had a plan for me. Because, all of those doubts and feelings would disappear when I would tell my negative voice to shut up and I would share my experience of God's love with people. The overwhelming tangible love I felt in heaven would come washing over me. The more I shared God's love and purpose with people the more I felt like the heavely me was being reveled on earth.

There would be times I would want my story to be like everyone else's. It was like I left the matrix of this world and had seen the truth and knew that I could never be content with anything less than the truth of who God had called me to be. There were times when I wished I could forget and disappear into anonymity because of my feelings of unworthiness. Though I had many questions, I never turned down the opportunity to pray with anyone. I was in a huge amount of physical pain, but when I was talking to someone about heaven and Jesus, all the pain would fade away. It was amazing!

Although I was a Christian and believed in heaven and hell, there was a little part of me that secretly thought gold streets and mansions in heaven sounded like a fairytale. Before my experience, I could never imagine being there in a real way. My daughter Amanda said once that she had a dream that she was raptured into heaven only to find her family was not there. She wandered around looking for us in a panic. This is the heaven I had previously imagined.

I could not understand how we could be happy in heaven knowing that we had missed an opportunity to bring our loved ones with us. How could I wake up on golden streets in my amazing mansion and be happy knowing that someone I knew might have been in hell burning for all eternity? I knew that what I learned in heaven was that I needed to be God's hug to people on earth.

I still had many questions about my experience when I came back. So, I asked the questions that were burdening me about my time in heaven and one by one God gave me the answers.

SIX
GOOGLING GOD AND PULLING WEEDS

Toward the end of my recovery, I was getting weary, and I started spending hours on the computer googling my ailments and trying to answer my own questions, even the ones I knew were not on Google. I was asking Google questions only God could answer. I had been praying and hearing from God about other people, but not for me. I was still worried about the stuff I was personally going through.

So, I laid out all my questions for God and one-by-one started getting answers in different ways. It was either through His Word, peaceful words in my spirit, dreams, revelations from events, or after pondering the Word of God. One by one, I would get the answers that would lead me to write this book.

The Lord's initial answer was clear, "You can't Google God, just ask Me."

I do not know if you can imagine how stupid I felt, at that moment.

How do I ask you God? His answer: Read, pray, worship, and listen.

Through doing exactly that, I got my answer on how to talk to God. So, I prayed, worshiped, and thought about God.

God Answers My Questions

"Why didn't I know my family when I first got to heaven? Why did I have no memory of them initially?"

In that still quiet voice that we spoke about earlier, the Holy Spirit answered me, "I blot out your sins because My grace is sufficient." I realized it would be a sin for me not to reach as many as I could.

"What did Jesus look like?"

God answered, "Like you when you are deep in worship."

"What did You mean when You showed me the world and gave me the choice to come back? What did You mean when You said, "If you go back, you'll have to go through something?"

There was no doubt I was going through something! As I was reading the Bible while in the hospital, I kept reading about healing. I saw that Jesus went about healing people in all different ways instantly. There was never a spot in the Bible where Jesus said, "check back with me in six months." There was obviously something holding me back that God wanted to identify so I could be free of it.

And then I realized that the something I was going through had something to do with the time it was going to take me to understand how valuable I was to God and how much he loved me.

I asked, **"Lord, why did I have to go through some things?"**

And in my spirit, He answered, "**You had weeds in your garden**."

I asked, "What weeds and how do I get rid of these weeds?"

And again, in my spirit He answered, "You can Google that!" I believe God has a sense of humor.

So, I did. I got on the computer and googled how to get rid of weeds. The answer was basically, "Pull weeds up by their roots but leave the soil." It was a metaphor for my soul.

Instructions for Pulling Weeds Applied to My Soul

1. Kill weeds at their roots but leave the soil. Once we discover the weed, we need to kill it. I discovered the weeds God was talking about were the lies I had been believing all my life. To kill these weeds, I had to start by not giving Satan the glory by focusing on the lie instead of focusing on the victory over the lie. I spent a lot of time telling people how I survived things. I would give God credit for saving me. However, I was still allowing Satan to push my buttons and having to overcome the same lies repeatedly.

In the book of Genesis, Satan convinced Eve that the truth was a lie by twisting God's words and making God seem like He was trying to keep something from her. Satan's goal was to steal God's throne and take away our potential. He wanted to destroy God's family unit. Satan knows that if we understand where the lies come from in our past, we can unravel them and unleash our true potential.

God must slow me down at times and make me lay down in green pastures. I spend too much time thinking about what I could be doing or what I should have done, causing me to worry and lose sleep. God designed you and me to subdue the land, to have dominion over our environment, and to be helpers. Worry and sleepless nights originate in thoughts that do not focus on what God has told us to think on.

> *Finally, brethren, whatever things are true, whatever things are noble, whatever things are just, whatever things are pure, whatever things are lovely, whatever things are of good report, if there is any virtue and if there is anything praiseworthy—* ***meditate on these things*** (Philippians 4:8 NKJV emphasis added).

When Adam and Eve were in the Garden, they were presented with a lie that was deceptive and went against what God had taught them. The lie might have been passed on by Eve, who had been deceived, but it originated from Satan. Satan did not blatantly tell her to eat this fruit and go against God. He said what he usually says, "Did God really say?" She was asked a question which she answered. Then he planted a thought which was a lie. It was a lie that would derail humanity. Adam and Eve had a choice to take control of that lie, capture it, and kill it. However, because they did not capture and kill it, it captured and killed them, and all they could have been. Humanity would be enslaved because of that lie until Jesus came and set things straight.

When God came to walk in the Garden of Eden and found Adam and Eve trying to hide in shame, covering themselves with fig leaves because they were naked, He said to Adam, **"Who told you, you were naked?"** God did not ask the question because He had taken the day off and was confused about who was out to deceive Adam and Eve. He did not ask because He needed to know the answer to the question. He was making a point.

God had made Adam and Eve to live a good life in the Garden of Eden. He wanted Adam to identify who told them a lie that made them start thinking that way. God knew the answer was Satan. God had given Adam and Eve a choice to believe it or not. They chose wrong and lost their birthright. Jesus came into the world to give us a choice to believe in Him as our Savior and to get our birthright back.

The thoughts and ideas we adopt as true and believe in can be our saving grace or our destruction. We can walk around loving the Lord, proclaiming to be Christians, but still walk around in bondage because Satan sold us a stinking lie and we believed it. Once you have discovered the lies in your life, the ones that separate you from who God says you are, it is time to kill that lie and pull it up by the root.

The next instruction says to leave the soil. I believe this means that even though we have killed the lie at the root, we need to understand that there will always be lies living deep in the soil waiting to turn up. Understanding that the enemy will bombard us with lies daily shows us we need to be on guard by knowing who we are in Christ. It is time to play offense instead of defense. As we travel down life's path, we are bound to stir up the dirt where sleeping weeds lie. The secret is don't even entertain them.

2. Apply Mulch: What is mulch? According to Wikipedia, mulch is a layer of material applied to the surface of the soil. The reasons for applying mulch include conservation of soil moisture, improving fertility and health of the soil, reducing weed growth, and enhancing the visual appeal of the area. It is a covering that is intended to protect from damage or injury.

Spiritually, when I thought of mulch, I felt it represented my Christian friends and my church fellowship. I needed to learn from more seasoned Christians, listen to their testimonies, and filter what they say through the Word of God to learn the lessons of spiritual warfare that would protect me. In this way, I could avoid the trouble altogether without having to go through the battle. This meant seeking godly wisdom through God's people. We are never alone.

> *Hebrews 10:25 reminds us, "Let us not neglect our meeting together, as some people do, but encourage one another" (NLT).*

The devil loves to pick us off one at a time when we are alone. He loves to separate us through offenses, opinions, social media, and politics.

We need to know the weapons of warfare that are available to us through God's word (see Ephesians 6:10-18) and the agreement with God's people. In Matthew 18:20, Jesus said, "For where two or three are gathered together in My name, I am there in the midst of them" (NKJV). Don't go into the enemy's camp alone or without your spiritual armor.

3. Lop off Their Heads: It's easy to make a garden look good by taking a weed eater to it and lopping off the tops of the weeds or taking a pair of scissors and just cutting them down.

Unfortunately, the root is still there. Even though it may seem pleasant for a moment, unless you go for the roots you will see weeds again after the first rain. A good example of this is in our relationships. Our whole life is made up of relationships. How we are treated by those people and respond greatly affects our happiness. How well we do in life is always interdependent on other people. You may feel that you did not get the love you deserved in your last relationship. You may feel your new relationship is going great, but something happens, and those old feelings of rejection creep up and you react to the new situation in a stronger way than you would have if this had been the first time. It might not seem fair to the person you just unleashed on, but what is happening is they just dug up an old root.

Lots of times, there are underlying problems and destructive pathways that we have developed from past relationships or from past hurts that have carried over into our new relationships. Often, we put our best foot forward, looking and acting the part. This may make a relationship seem wonderful at first, but the first time there is a problem or a hard rain, the roots that were buried pop up as weeds overnight.

Ephesians 4:26-27 advises us, "When angry, do not sin;

do not ever let your wrath (your exasperation, your fury or indignation) last until the sun goes down. Leave no [such] room *or* foothold for the devil [give no opportunity to him]" (AMPC).[2]

Hebrews 12:14-16 says, "Strive to live in peace with everybody and pursue that consecration *and* holiness without which no one will [ever] see the Lord. Exercise foresight *and* be on the watch to look [after one another], to see that no one falls back from *and* fails to secure God's grace (His unmerited favor and spiritual blessing), in order that no **root of resentment** (rancor, bitterness, or hatred) shoots forth and causes trouble *and* bitter torment, and the many become contaminated *and* defiled by it)" (AMPC emphasis added).[3]

4. Mind the Gaps Between Plants. Weeds grow where good things are not planted. If you don't know what the Word of God says is the truth, the enemy can come in and plant a lie in an open space. I found out that lies like weeds are never invited into a garden. They either come in where other things are not

---

[2] Amplified Bible, Classic Edition (AMPC)

[3] Amplified Bible, Classic Edition (AMPC)

planted, or they are sent into the garden by oncoming winds and association with the plants nearby.

The first way weeds came in was where God's Word was not planted in our hearts and minds. Sometimes, it is brought on by our thought processes, our association with people we grew up with, and ideas that we had accepted as truth. In John 8:32, Jesus explained, "And you shall know the truth, and the truth shall make you free" (NKJV). If you don't understand or know the promises of God in His Word concerning you, then you can't be set free. Satan loves to attack children because they do not know who they are yet. Some of us remain children never knowing who we are or what God our Creator says about us.

There are certain truths that our heart needs to know. We need to ask ourselves:

1. *What is the lie that I have battled?*
2. *Where did the lie begin?*
3. *Do I need healing?*
4. *What is the truth of God?*
5. *What is the promise of God that will defeat this lie?*
6. *Do I believe that Promise is true and applies to me?*
7. *Stand on the promise by saying and adopting it as your own.*

Ask the Holy Spirit to lead you in truth in order to lop off the enemy's head with the truth of the Word of God.

5. Water and feed the plants you want, not the weeds. If you had a garden full of beautiful roses and you saw weeds coming up, it would make sense to pull the weeds and water the roses. Can you imagine going out to the garden and ignoring the roses and feeding the weeds instead? We do just that when we feed lies through self-talk. It is important to listen to what you are telling yourself. Are you saying things like: I'm fat, ugly, not smart enough, my hair is wrong, I am not worthy, I am unlovable, I am always last, I am always overlooked, my life is wrong, I cannot quit doing drugs, I can't quit smoking, I can't write a book?

I have written a lot of honest prayers to God in my journal asking Him to show me how to fix things. Sometimes, I go back and read old journals and realize the lie I was laboring under at the time. Begin to speak the promises of God over yourself. Write good things that God says about who you are in your journal. Practice saying them out loud in the mirror until it's the first thought that comes up when you hear something negative cross your mind. I used to teach in a cosmetology school, and I would always tell my students that in order to learn something, you need to see it, read it, write it, say it, and do it.

Here are some examples of what God says about you to declare over yourself:

> *I am beautifully and wonderfully made* (Psalm 139:14 NKJV).
>
> *I can do all things through Christ* (Philippians 4:13 NKJV).
>
> *I have power and love and a sound mind* (2 Timothy 1:7 NKJV).
>
> *Goodness follows me all the days of my life* (Psalm 23:6 NKJV).

6. Use a Chemical and Kill the Weeds. Some people get rid of weeds in the garden with chemicals. Chemicals will slow weeds down but may leave roots that will bring back more weeds. Did you ever notice that weeds seem to just pop up after a rain? We all have storms in our lives, and we can bury our problems in drugs, alcohol, and even prescription drugs. In my case, I used sugar, caffeine, and medication to help mask my underlying problem. However, when I had a storm in my life, I found I was facing all the same problems over again. I had never gotten to the root of the problem.

Chemicals don't heal, they treat temporarily. I don't want you to think that I am putting down taking prescribed medications to help with depression, anxiety, or ADD. You have to start where you are at. I believe God wants to heal you, but He gave doctors wisdom to work in their calling to help you treat your problem and to make it manageable for your benefit. This is an area that you will have to make some decisions on for yourself between you and God.

In my case, I had too many weeds to believe in my healing and there was not enough medication in the world to make the underlying pain go completely away. I had too many lies planted firmly in my life to even begin to say, "Okay, I won't take any medication to help me with the symptoms." God gave doctors wisdom and gave them the tools to help us, so get help if you need it.

However, God says come as you are, and I will defeat the devourer for you. You need to understand that God loves you and He can and wants to help you. There are plenty of people who love the Lord who He may send to you, who can be your covering and help you fight the battle and help you through it.

James 1:5-6 says, "If any of you lacks wisdom, let him ask of God, who gives to all liberally and without reproach, and it will be given to him. But let him ask in faith, with no doubt, for he who doubts is like a wave of the sea driven and tossed by the wind" (NKJV).

7. Put a Barrier Cloth Down and Replant the Garden. Some gardens were planted on top of weeds and as long as the garden is in that area there are going to be weeds. This has to do with associations. We sometimes must put some distance between us and our old associations. If you have a problem with drinking, you probably do not need to hang out with the guys at the bar after work. If I am dieting, the first thing I do is try to clean out the pantry of any potential temptations. Putting a barrier down in the garden is about distancing ourselves from areas we know we are weak in. Sometimes, it's people that know how to push our buttons. Some gardens are so riddled with weeds, that they have to be totally cleared out, a weed guard put down, and a whole new garden planted. Some people are so riddled with weeds that we need to totally differentiate ourselves from them and put down a whole new foundation. Spiritually, this may mean evaluating the foundation you have built your belief system upon. Jesus told a parable about a good foundation in Matthew 7:24-27.

> *Therefore whoever hears these sayings of Mine, and does them, I will liken him to a wise man who built his house on the rock: and the rain descended, the floods came, and the winds blew and beat on that house; and it did not fall, for it was founded on the rock. But everyone who hears these sayings of Mine, and does not do them, will be like a foolish man who built his house on the sand: and the rain descended, the floods came, and the winds blew and beat on that house; and it fell. And great was its fall* (Matthew 7:24-27 NKJV).

8. Pull the Weeds by Hand. The next way to remove weeds in my research said to just simply pull them out by hand. However, if you have ever pulled weeds on a sunny day, you probably ripped your hands up trying to get all the roots out. You must get the weed and all its roots out or it comes back almost immediately. My way to try to do this with the weeds in my life was to read a lot of self-help books and try to figure out how I could engineer my way into healthy thinking. I read books on dating, codependency, depression, weight loss, nutrition, diets, exercise, God, and spirituality. I collected magazines with fad diets hoping I would find the truth somewhere. When I wasn't reading books, I was going to school.

One time, the bank called me because I had bought so many books at Barnes and Noble, they thought it was fraud. Do not get me wrong. I am a fan of reading. I hope you are too. I was learning from other believers through reading, and I was planting good promise seeds, but maybe there were also some weeds. I say this because I was not filtering what I was reading through the Word of God to make sure it was solid advice. I had no idea what was real truth or what was not real or where it had originated. I have learned since, that many good truths are mulched up and recirculated as original ideas. These truths work because they were based on the Word of God in the first place. I prefer now to fact-check what I read by seeing if what I am reading has a scriptural component.

So, what is the answer?

"So, Lord," I asked. "How do I get rid of the weeds? It seems I had been trying to pull weeds for a long time, but every time a storm comes, the weeds of self-doubt, anxiety, depression, condemnation, and fear come back up."

The Lord answered me, "With rainy days."

I asked, "Lord, I do not understand. If it's not pulling the weeds by hand, if it's not moving the garden, if using chemicals on the garden doesn't completely get the weeds out, if me going to church every Sunday and Wednesday, and serving as a pastor did not do it, then how do you get rid of the weeds? How do I get rid of the weeds in my life that are keeping me from my healing and keeping me from peace of mind?"

I could feel the Lord smile on me at that moment and He said, "That's easy! Your life is a garden, and it will always need tending. It's okay to disassociate if you need to and it's okay to read a good book on the subject if you go to the Word and it lines up. It's okay to go to the doctor and ask for help and it is okay to go to people who have already struggled with the same problems and have come to Me with their questions and won."

As I prayed and listened to the Lord, I sensed Him say, "The best way to get rid of the weeds is through the rain. After a good rain, the ground is soaked, and weeds are pulled up easily, root and all. In other words, through the watering of the Word and through the renewing of your mind, you can pull the weeds out once and for all easily. It is not hard on you and the weeds will be gone. Then plant a promise from Me where the weed used to be."

This was an amazing picture for me of where I was mentally at the time. I had weeds in my garden. You see, I could not believe God could heal me because I had such low self-worth. I didn't believe He wanted to. I was acting like an employee of God instead of a daughter. I was working so hard at earning my way to heaven by gathering all my self-worth from what I did for other people instead of who God showed me I was in His Word and who I was in heaven.

The truth I learned from all my "Googling" was God wants to fulfill His promises to us. He is our Dad. The best picture of this is becoming a parent.

No matter how old my kids get, they are still my kids. My grown children come straight into my house and get food and eat and go rest in my bed. They are welcome. Most of the time, they walk straight in and head to the refrigerator and look for something to eat. They do not ask permission. As far as I am concerned, it is as much theirs as it is mine. I love them and I want them to have it. It does my heart good to know that we have a good relationship, and they know that I want them to have it. I do not ask them to pay me back or ask for money for that soda they just got out of the refrigerator. They don't ask how much they need to work to get what I have to offer them.

They are my kids; I love them and there is nothing I won't give them if it is good for them. God loves us and is a good Dad.

Reaping the Harvest

I began to live in a new truth about the promises of God. The truth was I did not have to live with illness, anxiety, sickness, and simply surviving as I waited for the other shoe to fall. I did not have to feel that every time I had a calamity that it was God's will for me to survive it, so it would be a testimony. You see, Jesus already went to the cross so I did not have to.

Finally, I got hold of the truth of God's grace. I could live victoriously. God's grace had always been there waiting for me to take advantage of, but I was not understanding it. I learned through God's love that it was time for me to let God's grace be sufficient for me. It was my job to talk about Jesus and to point to His testimony. It occurred to me that I had been living one tragedy after another under the guise of making lemonade out of lemons for the glory of God. It never occurred to me that I didn't have to have the lemons (limits) in the first place.

I was a full-time receiver of what Satan would send my way, never once thinking that God would protect me if I asked Him to. I also needed to understand that if you stand in the middle of the street, you might get hit. I needed to ask God about some of the decisions I was making in my life that were putting me in harm's way.

Ask Yourself...

1. *What is the lie that I have battled?*
2. *Where did the lie begin?*
3. *Do I need healing?*
4. *What is the truth of God?*
5. *What is the promise of God that will defeat this lie?*
6. *Do I believe that promise pertains to me?*
7. *Listen for and pray for a word from the Lord on your situation.*
8. *Once you hear from the Lord, make the promises of God your foundation for your belief and stand on it by speaking over your situation.*

Once you have discovered the lies in your life, the ones that separate you from who God says you are, it is time to kill those lies and pull them up by the root.

Lots of times there are underlying problems and destructive pathways we developed from past relationships or from past hurts that carry over into our new relationships.

SEVEN
WHY DID I HAVE TO DIE IN THE FIRST PLACE?

The question of why I had to die in the first place was another nagging question in my mind. Surely, I could have learned some other way, why this and why now in my life. When I got out of the hospital my husband encouraged me to build up my strength by going to a Christian Women's Conference. I could barely walk up the stairs and it was going to be a nature trip. I was not excited. The last nature trip I had been on like that was with a sales group, where I had won a contest, but I arrived too late to accept the award due to traffic. I was told by the presenters at the conference that I had set a bad example and was told to rethink my steps. I was angry and quit the sales group after that. I did not know where we would be going on this trip, but it was in the same vicinity as that one and I was remembering my bitterness. It was obviously something I was holding on to or I would not have been thinking about it, years later. I was so surprised when we rounded the corner and were at the exact same place. I was staying in the same house and sitting in the same living room. I knew that I needed to forgive and settled down for a quiet moment to reflect on this teachable moment.

I love to keep notes on things, so I write in journals constantly; sometimes not in the same one, just what's available. I opened an old journal which I had grabbed quickly when I left my house. I opened it to write down my feelings and noticed that two pages were written in it. I considered ripping the pages out because the two pages seemed of little consequence. I decided to stop and read the pages before I threw them away. After reading the date and what I had written on these pages I had my answer to why did I have to die in the first place. The night before I was to have my original laminectomy surgery, I was visiting my daughter who had given birth that day. I was super excited about my new grandson. As I stumbled through the hospital having to face all the relatives and feeling like a sad sight, I thought to myself, how did I ever get to this place in my life. All my feelings of unworthiness were weighing on me. I felt a lot of anger at myself and my situation. I did not want to face the consequences of all the weight I had let myself gain or the long hours I chose to work despite a bad back. A lot was on my mind about the surgery the next day. It seemed in one part of my life, I had everything good happening, yet I felt I was risking my life to have this surgery which the doctor was considering an emergency for my symptoms. I was scared that I was looking at the family I might be leaving behind. In the hospital gift shop, they had journals, so I bought one to air my feelings out. I wrote an angry prayer to God in that journal. I had a friend who had the same gastric bypass surgery as me. She had all the same symptoms and back problems. Her story was scarily like mine, medically. She ended up dying in a rehab facility, crippled and alone.

So, the two-page prayer I wrote in that journal that night before my surgery was written just prior to my dying. In it was the following excerpt….

> *"Dear God,*
>
> *I have done everything that a good Christian should do. I have prayed. I have served. I have given my time and my money. I have named and claimed*

my healing, and yet, here I am, the night before my surgery, and You have not healed me. I guess I am going to have to face my worst fear...death!"

There it was! The answer. **I had written down and believed in my own death.** I had not realized until that day back at the camp, that God had not forsaken me. He did not want me to die. I had declared with my own words that I would face my worst fear—I would die. He had in fact caught me! Despite my words and the backward faith wherein I declared my own death, God intervened and pulled me aside. He showed me He was real, he showed me who I was, and what I would be leaving behind, and his ultimate purpose for my life. Through God's grace and because of the heartfelt request of my husband and children, He gave me a choice to come back, change, and introduce Him to the world through my newfound filter of God's love. He showed us all this love through Jesus dying on the cross for our sins so we would never have to be separated from Him again.

God Showed Me What I Needed to See

Still, I had a few more questions. I knew why I had to die in the first place, but I wondered why He showed me a perfect version of me. So, I asked the Lord:

"Why did you show me this beautiful, perfect woman and then send me back to this sick, fat, tired, still in pain one? Why do I have to wait to be that beautiful woman?"

God showed me the one thing I needed to see, and I must remind myself of it daily. He showed me my true identity. **"Why do I have to wait to be that woman?"** I'd asked Him. At the time it seemed like a cruel joke. Physically, I was not the woman I saw. Emotionally? Well, I was growing.

The Lord answered me in my spirit, "Danielle, you do not have to wait to be that woman. I didn't show you who you're going to be, I showed you who you are! This is who you are. You are beautifully and wonderfully made, you are not a mistake, you are not lacking in any way. Your physical body is just a shell. It is the temple of the Holy Spirit, and you should take care of it because it is precious. You need to keep it strong so that you can do the work you were sent to do on Earth. It is your purpose to love people with My love and to point them to Me so that I can show them that love. You can reach all those people that I showed you while you were in heaven, but make no mistake Danielle, you are that girl, you are that woman. You are a woman who is wonderfully and masterfully made."

Every day, I need to remind myself that I am more than the

bad things that have happened to me, my aging body, my aches and pains, my good days or my bad. I am more than what looks back at me in the mirror. I am more than people's opinions of me. I am loved deeply by my heavenly Father, the Creator of the universe. I am His daughter, and I am made in His image.

I am sure to most of you this would have been a good enough answer, but not for me. I still had more questions.

"**Why didn't I get to see Jesus?" I asked.** You see in my mind, if I had gotten to see Jesus, I would have come back and beaten all those non-believers over the head with it. I could have confirmed that He was our Savior, the one true living God.

And in deep prayer and in my spirit The Lord asked, "Danielle, what day did you die?"

So, I looked it up. To my surprise, I had died on Father's Day. I had been swimming in God's great big, huge hug on Father's Day! I had been with the Heavenly Father on Father's Day, engulfed in His all white, beautiful, glorious light, overflowing with love. I was with my Heavenly Father on Father's Day, and God had given me a choice to come back to fulfill His purpose on earth and change my life forever.

God grants us forgiveness and grace beyond measure.

Why didn't I remember my family until after God told me I had a family?

After much prayer and soul searching. I feel the reason I didn't know my friends and family in the beginning, is because God's grace is in fact, sufficient for us. We could never live-in heaven looking back and knowing that there is a heaven and there is a hell (a place that was never meant for us) and having the knowledge that there were people that our Lord and Savior Jesus Christ gave His life for that we did not reach out to or that there are those that were given the truth of God and denied Him, facing a judgement that was not meant for them. Jesus paid the price for our sins with His blood 2000 years ago giving us the victory over sin. We are all left with a choice to make: to decide where we will spend eternity.

> *Death has been swallowed up in victory. Where, O death, is your victory? Where, O death, is your sting? Thanks be to God! He gives us the victory through our Lord Jesus Christ* (1 Corinthians15:54b-57 NIV).

Death in Adam, Life in Christ

Therefore, just as sin entered the world through one man, and death through sin, so also death was passed on to all men because all sinned. For sin was in the world before the law was given, but sin is not taken into account when there is no law. Nevertheless, death reigned from Adam until Moses, even over those who did not sin in the way that Adam transgressed. He is a pattern of the One to come. But the gift is not like the trespass. For if the many died by the trespass of the one man, how much more did God's grace and the gift that came by the grace of the one man, Jesus Christ, abound to the many! Again, the gift is not like the result of one man's sin: The judgment that followed one sin brought condemnation, but the gift that followed many trespasses brought justification. For if, by the trespass of the one man, death reigned through that one man, how much more will those who receive an abundance of grace and the gift of righteousness reign in life through the one man, Jesus Christ! So then, just as one

> *trespass brought condemnation for all men, so one act of righteousness brought justification and life for all men. For just as through the disobedience of one man (ADAM) the many were made sinners, so also through the obedience of the one man (JESUS CHRIST) the many will be made righteous.*
>
> *The law came in so that the trespass would increase; but where sin increased, grace increased all the more, so that, just as sin reigned in death, so also grace might reign through righteousness to bring eternal life through Jesus Christ our Lord* (Romans 5:12-21 Berean Study Bible).[4]

Take a moment to reflect on what I was beginning to learn after I experienced My Journey to Heaven about God's plan and purpose for all of us. We can be ensnared by our own words. We are made in the image of God who spoke the world into existence and gave us dominion. Therefore, it would behoove us to know the promises of God and His goodwill for us so that we can speak with godly authority. How does this revelation affect the way you speak about yourself and others?

---

[4] Public Domain

EIGHT
MY HIDDEN BUTTONS

It wasn't all spiritual sunshine and roses in the hospital. There were certain people in my life who knew how to push my buttons. Okay, I will say it, it's my mom. My mother had never gotten the concept that unsolicited advice was criticism. She would lead with a statement like, "You are awesome, but...." It was what came after the "but" that always canceled out the first part of the sentence. These conversations were never invited. It was like a rite of passage for Mom. Oh, I am sure that there were a few other people like that in my life, but she already knows she pushes my buttons and doesn't mind me using her as an example.

So I found out that no matter what, walking in love was

easier with strangers than with people that I knew, especially my mother. I realized I had a lot of past hurts that were like hidden buttons waiting to be pushed. I had a lot of buttons that could be pushed and I learned that loving strangers who would come into my room was easier than loving people who I had a history with. Although, it seemed like I should have been able to magically draw a line between the old me and the new one, I was working things out with God. It was not instantaneous.

Months after being in the hospital, my mother *finally* came up to the hospital for a couple of days to give Jim a break. This was already a problem because I felt like she was late. The hurt was already there, like a button waiting to be pushed by the enemy. She was really trying. In fact, she was overworking herself trying to help. She locked me in my bed like I was six and asked lots of questions to everyone about my care. I was resentful that it had taken months for her to come and see me. In my mind, she was months too late to show me she cared.

The hospital staff and I had already developed a sort of rhythm. Everyone knew me and I knew them. In my mind, my mom was making waves where she should not interfere. I just wanted her to sit quietly and read a magazine or something. However, that was not my mother. She was always bigger than life and she sucked the air out of the room. She was always trying to be the center of attention.

To be fair, mom had been the oldest of ten children and they were all her half-siblings. She was the only child between her father and mother who had divorced when she was young and had children with their subsequent spouses. So, in both families, she was the odd man out. She was always lacking attention and love in her own life. This had caused her to be an unfinished symphony in her life and sort of a vacuum of need.

To make matters worse, she had been unsuccessful in relationships. She was missing something in her life that would make her covet what was in yours. She had a bigger than life personality. It could be the attention you were getting, your relationships, or the clothes you were wearing. It did not matter what it was, if you had it, she deserved it. Later in life, realizing she had a problem that she was working on with the Lord, she began to refer to herself as the covet queen.

It was not the first time I had been in the hospital in my life. She would come to the hospital under the pretense of taking care of me. Almost every time, my mom would find a reason to leave my bedside, get suddenly ill, and end up in the emergency room getting herself checked in. One time, she made a big deal that we should be in the same hospital room. I began to realize it was an attention thing.

Memories flashed in my mind of the past when she had come to the hospital to help me. I was concerned she would end up in a bed right beside me, or down the hall, or in the ER. These memories of mom making a scene flooded in like a Tsunami when she came up to see me in the hospital. It was like post-traumatic stress syndrome. All the love in heaven that I had been overflowing with, seemed to fly out the window almost instantly when she arrived.

This time, what pushed my button was the roses. She had gotten me roses. She went on and on about how I better keep those roses and have them dried. She'd better see them in my house so when she died, I would remember her. I got angry and thought, how terrible it was of her to miss the point that I had died. I thought about how we had to be talking about her and her death.

I started to fume inside as the next three days dragged on. I had been in the hospital for months and I had died, but instead of talking about that, she wanted me to talk about her. Frankly, she was driving me crazy. In the back of my mind, memories of how she had insisted that I carry roses from my father's casket around with me for years and how sad that had made me was all I could think of. I finally could not hold on to my thoughts any longer and decided to tell her I would take a picture of the roses, but I would not keep the dead roses forever. She got furious and went over and dumped the still fresh roses and the vase in the garbage. I wanted to get up and leave the room, but I was locked in my hospital bed like a six-year-old.

My mother and I have always had a strained relationship. She seems to know how to push all my buttons and remembers all my shortcomings, the real ones and the ones she has made up in her mind about me. I was so frustrated and fed up. So taking a stand for myself, I asked her to leave the hospital. I said as nicely as I could that she was stressing me out. I felt that since I was the one in the hospital, I should be the one that got my way. I thought, how dare she come up here and pick a fight with me and aggravate me when I was clearly fighting for my life. My mother was pushing all my buttons and now I was done. She angrily packed up and went downstairs to wait for a ride to leave.

Conviction

Once she was gone, I could hear the Holy Spirit yelling in my ear, "Where's your unconditional love now?" I could feel the empathy of the Holy Spirit recognizing her pain and I knew that the only way she could ever realize what I had experienced was real was if I could move past our history and give her the love that she was so desperately seeking. I immediately had remorse for the situation and wanted to go down and stop her, but I was locked in my bed. When I finally got a nurse's attention, she took the opportunity to give me medication while she was in the room, and she unlocked my bed. Then, a doctor doing rounds came in to discuss my care.

Just when it seemed like it was going to be a train wreck, my husband came in, so I gave him a quick rundown of my situation and sent him to go and get her. He did and she came back up. While I was alone and he was going to get her, I prayed, "God, please help me not to say anything in word or do anything in deed to instigate anything."

This meant no deep sighs, no rolling of my eyes, making eye contact, and not telling her to stop asking questions and making condescending statements. Yes, I was guilty of doing all these things in the past. I wish I could tell you that with the Holy Spirit's help, I instantly had words of love and wisdom for my mother. However, all I had was the knowledge of what I would say if I opened my mouth, so I tried to keep my mouth shut while she was there, praying silently. The Holy Spirit was reminding me and whispering in my ear, "Love, Love, Love."

I apologized and smiled, but for two days we hardly spoke. However, we did not fight, and she went home feeling good about herself and left in a peaceful fashion. It taught me a valuable lesson about depending on the Holy Spirit for everything. When I would feel anger rise up in me, I would pray, and it would pass. When I started letting her take care of me and feel important, she calmed down and she apologized. I have always allowed my mother to be a stumbling block in my life. I would react to her and participate in every argument, like a puppet on a string. I say participate because I realized I have a choice on whether to participate.

We all have a choice to participate in an argument. The Holy Spirit revealed in those days that all her jabs were a result of her pain and the things she had experienced in her life. If she seemed jealous, angry, or acted neglected it was because she felt a void and a lack of love in her life. People who are hurting and empty can become need vacuums sucking up the joy around them and spewing anger, frustration, and hurt. If we are not mindful, we can get sucked in. I guess what I have learned is to stay off the floor, rise above and get my head in a heavenly place.

I was learning that when people are at their worst,
That is when they need Jesus the most.

I tried only to speak in love, concentrating on positive things and speaking about happy things. I decided to follow a strong dance leader, God. He leads in love. I have started to decipher the difference between love and emotion. Love is stable and never takes anything. Emotion is like a roller coaster that is up one minute down the next. I have come to realize that I can't change my mother. No amount of talking, arguing, or even explaining to her about how I feel can change her or change how she deals with things. This was freeing to me to finally understand. I could finally love my mother without having a condition for how she would act.

I found a new superpower, it's called prayer. I prayed for her, and I prayed for myself. I asked God to help me to see her through His eyes and let me have the proper response; the one He would want me to have. In other words, I have learned that we cannot change how other people treat us, only how we respond. In my mother's case, I could not change her actions, only my reactions.

My ability to act differently did not come from a psychology book, although I had read many of them. The power finally came when I allowed the Holy Spirit to lead me in a love dance. I have already noticed a difference in our relationship. It is funny to me that since I have changed how I respond, she has started to seek God and started to deal internally with some of her behaviors. She has begun the process of healing from her own past hurts allowing her to act differently. In the past, the arguments we would have would steer us away from the healing process and instead, put the focus on the argument.

I asked the Lord what to do with this knowledge and revelation that I received from my time in heaven. We are to filter everything we do through unconditional love. However, if you try to do it on your own, you will find it is impossible! It is only through a deep, close, daily relationship with God that this can be accomplished. You must first receive and understand His magnificent unconditional love for you, then you can give that love to others. Let me assure you, you are loveable! Jesus loves you so he went to the cross for you!

NINE
THE LOVE DANCE

The reason I called this chapter the love dance is because I can't dance. Let me correct myself. I can fling myself around on the dance floor, but it wouldn't amount to much. I seem to have always had two left feet. Dancing is something that requires all of your attention. I always felt awkward and my dad who had won contests dancing, always told me that I needed a strong leader on the dance floor. Not unlike my awkwardness on the dance floor, my ability to love people was challenging me, too. It seems that what I had the least of in my life was trust. To me no love was unconditional.

It was not that I was not loved by my family. It was that I

felt that love was a payment for something I did right. Since I was not sure I was lovable, I did not think I could do anything right. So, I did not trust enough to give love freely.

All the love that I was able to give in the hospital came straight from the Holy Spirit. My experience in heaven was overflowing with love. I had God's love all over me. It did not seem to matter who came into my room or if I knew them well or not. I would delve into conversations about their day and their life, what made them happy, and what made them sad. I was interested instead of interesting.

Although I had always seen myself as a person that loved people, there was always a part of me that needed them to love me back. Love to me was transactional. This new love was not transactional, it was just because. True love was loving someone who may never even know you existed and who had nothing to offer you. My heart went out to them and all I wanted to do was to pass on what God had given me, His unconditional love. It was because I now knew love could fix anything and everything. Homelessness, world hunger, and world peace could all be fixed with God's love.

I still remember the feeling of overwhelming love in heaven. I stood there as the waves of love washed over me, washing away and filling the empty holes in my heart. I sound like an angel don't I. Well, I hate to burst your bubble, but I am human, and I still do have past hurts and memories that I deal with. What I had not dealt with was about to teach me a big lesson in loving no matter what.

Learning to Dance with My Husband

I was praying for there to be better communication between me and my husband and the Lord kept telling me one thing. "When you learn to dance with your husband, you will be okay." That was funny because I had danced with my father plenty of times, but whenever I tried to dance with my husband, I had two left feet. I felt embarrassed. Jim would try to teach me, but it was not working. I had a friend named Carol who taught dance lessons and I asked her if she would teach us. I sent out a Facebook post with the amazing revelation I received as Jim and I learned ballroom dancing.

Through learning ballroom dancing, Jim is becoming a strong leader while I am learning how to be sensitive to His leading and not step on his toes. The Lord is really teaching us that the Holy Spirit should lead us in the dance of life.

Jim learned that he must move with his whole being. He must engage his core and move with his whole being making decisive steps toward his goal. When a man leads in a dance, it is a full-body movement. He must be fully engaged. He must navigate the room and move with firmness and grace because he is leading his partner. As his partner, I must be vigilant and equally engaged with all that I am anticipating his moves by being attentive to his every move, sensing which foot he will start on and which direction he intends to go. My form must mirror his with the exception of the tilt of my head which must be slightly to the side in order to allow him to survey the room and lead. In other words, ladies, I learned I had to get my own head out of the way. I must trust his every decision as I cannot see where we are going. I kept messing up because I would try to guess what he was going to do before he did it. The first thing the teacher taught me to do was to dance backward with my eyes closed and wait on him to shift his weight onto the foot he would move first. Then I would know my next move. This was a little scary, but ballroom dancing is an act of trust.

If you are wondering if I am still talking about the waltz, the answer is yes and no. In my marriage, I had to learn that my husband loved me and that I could trust him leading me. In my relationship with the Holy Spirit, it is the same.

Sometimes, I must get my head out of the way and let God lead, trusting that He loves me and wants what is best for me. When I can't see the end from the beginning, I trust God and go where He leads.

TEN
A WOMAN WITH A SWORD BY HER BED

For nearly two years, I tried to write this book about my life, only to find out from the editor that I had simply done a brain dump. Although it was necessary to do a brain dump, I felt as though I was back at square one trying to decide which of the millions of little miracles would be important for you to read. I was dragging my feet, overcome by the thoughts and the utter dread of rehashing all the negative things in my past. However, I was sure of one thing, God had not sent me back to sit and think, He sent me to do.

I happened to turn on one of my favorite preachers and they were talking about Queen Esther. Although my problem was not as serious as Queen Esther's, she too had to overcome her past and fulfill her purpose. Queen Esther had to risk her life to intervene for the lives of the Jewish people, who were going to be killed by her husband the King. He did not know that his own wife Esther, was in fact Jewish. Esther's uncle came to her and asked her to talk to her husband about sparing the Jewish people. She would have to tell her secret to her husband that she was a Jew. She knew that she was breaking the rules of going before her husband without being summoned and it would be his right to inflict the penalty of death.

Furthermore, once he heard what she had to say, it was not going to go over well. She had not been spoken to by her husband for 30 days and she wasn't sure he was wanting to speak to her. Her uncle said something very important. He said how do you know that you were not raised into this position for this very matter. He said trust me, if you don't stand up for God's people, then God will raise another in your family, and it is possible that you will perish.

What stood out to me in the story is we have a purpose we are meant to deliver, one way or another.

I knew two things, I had something to accomplish and the sword, the Word of God, was what was going to help me do it. Every morning I would wake and the words I would hear in my spiritual ear was a resounding I AM a woman with a sword by her bed. It sounded more like an epiphany to me than a fact. I didn't quite understand the meaning at first, only the resoluteness of the words rolling around in my head. As I began to seek God on the matter, the days that followed were full of questions and revelations. Does a sword fulfill its full purpose sitting by the bed? The answer is a resounding, No! The sword only fulfills its purpose in battle, and the living Word of God only fulfills its purpose if it is used for its purpose. I knew that I was given a choice in heaven to be here on task fulfilling my purpose. I had died and been given the choice to come back. Not just for my purpose, but for such a time as this: this time in a world where so many people question if God is real and if heaven is a real place. I realized I was holding back because I was afraid of ridicule. I was afraid of being different and of being disliked and unloved. I was wrong. God said we are the salt of the earth. We are aliens to this world.

> *Beloved, I beg you as sojourners and pilgrims, abstain from fleshly lusts which war against the soul, having your conduct honorable among the Gentiles, that when they speak against you as*

> *evildoers, they may, by your good works which they observe, glorify God in the day of visitation.* (1 Peter 2:11-12 ESV)

We are different and called out. Jesus said He did not come to bring peace to the world but to bring a sword.

> *"Do not think that I have come to bring peace to the earth. I have not come to bring peace, but a sword"* (Matthew 10:34 ESV).

> *"Think not that I am come to send peace on earth: I came not to send peace, but a sword. For I am come to set a man at variance against his father, and the daughter against her mother, and the daughter-in-law against her mother-in-law. And a man's foes shall be they of his household. He that loveth father or mother more than me is not worthy of me: and he that love son or daughter more than me is not worthy of me. And he that taketh not his cross, and follow after me, is not worthy of me. He that find his life shall lose it: and he that loses his life for my sake shall find it.* (Matthew 10:34-39 KJV)

> *And He said to him, "You shall love the Lord your God with all your heart, and with all your soul, and with all your mind"* (Matthew 22:37 ESV).

The Devil Is a Liar

I had to reconcile the past abuse in my life with my newfound love from the Lord and I had to unravel the lies of the enemy. I have heard all the lies of the enemy and lies that I perpetuated by telling them to myself.

Lies like I am inadequate, I'm not good enough, I'm ugly, fat, stupid, worthless, or simply not enough. Every time I hear lies like this, I want to stomp the enemy into the ground.

It's funny, all my life I knew the scripture that the enemy comes to steal, kill, and destroy. I took the words to mean it was a warning to watch out for Satan that he is out to get you. He was someone to be feared. Since I died, I see it differently. I now read the last part of the scripture. The scripture was not meant as a warning but a contrast.

> *"I am the gate. If anyone enters through Me, he will be saved. He will come in and go out and find pasture.* ***The thief comes only to steal and kill and destroy. I have come that they may have***

> ***life, and have it in all its fullness.*** *I am the good shepherd. The good shepherd lays down His life for the sheep"* (John 10:9-11 NIV).

Jesus is the good shepherd, and He has laid down His life for us. He has already fought the war and won. I do not have to live like a victim. God is not helpless to save me. The enemy has used people to do some awful things to me, but he has not defeated me. It was extremely hard to write this part of the book because I do not think of myself as a survivor or a victim of sexual abuse, but I did experience it and I do have victory over it, because of Jesus Christ. However, up until I died I did not know that. I thought God's only job was to pick me up when the devil was through with me. I felt helpless, worthless, and dirty. These lies were just tools that Satan used to steal my potential and convince me that I was powerless to overcome, to forgive, and to move passed the memories of my past. I have said once before that underlying pain is like a weed in your life ready to pop up at any given moment or a button waiting there for someone to push. I was walking around like a vending machine full of buttons waiting to be pushed and shocked at what would come up in me if I did not bury myself in a task to keep my mind off of it. I have stopped letting the enemy shock me and push my buttons. I have chosen not to have buttons.

How do you get rid of the buttons? You understand your attacker is Satan first, and he came to kill you and also to kill who you could have been, steal your peace of mind, and rob you in every way possible. Understand that Satan wants you to live your life looking backward and focusing on what he did to you. He wants to say it was not his fault but place blame on you for what happened to you or somebody else. He wants you to focus on hate, unforgiveness, blame, and loss. If you do that, then he will be stealing today's moment from you. The enemy wants you to live in the past and give you a new identity there. He wants you to say, I am a survivor.

Trust me, you are much more than a survivor; you are also a warrior, a winner, and a conqueror. While it can be freeing to admit to other women or counselors what you went through, the feelings you had when it happened, and to have a good cry over it. Once that is done, take those thoughts into captivity, kill them, give your heart and mind to the Lord, and worship your way through the battle in your mind. You have a new identity in Christ. The term "born again" is no accident. The old person with all the history, pain, and hurts must die and a new one is born through Jesus Christ. Draw a line in the sand every day to live in this day and this moment.

Although the memory of the incident is there, I can tell you now that I am whole in Christ, I do not walk around with the scarlet letter on my chest. I am new, my spirit is new, and my life is new. The devil likes to whisper in your ear and remind you of the trauma. Tell him to shut up. He knows the scripture, Jesus has you covered. You are not the sum of what has happened to you, you are not defined by your past failures and defeats or traumas. You are **more** than a conqueror through Christ Jesus. You are more!

> *Who shall separate us from the love of Christ? Shall trouble or distress or persecution or famine or nakedness or danger or sword? As it is written: "For Your sake we face death all day long; we are considered as sheep to be slaughtered." No, in all these things we are more than conquerors through Him who loved us* (Romans 8:35-37 NKJV).

> *I have been crucified with Christ, and I no longer live, but Christ lives in me. The life I live in the body, I live by faith in the Son of God, who*

> *loved me and gave Himself up for me* (Galatians 2:20 NIV).

Be Offensive, Not Defensive

If the devil does something to attack me, I attack him back. I like to pray out loud in my house or my car as I speak the promises of God about who I am. I sometimes turn up the worship music and dance in my living room. I look for opportunities to pray for other people or go out of my way to tell someone about Jesus. I send a clear message to Satan that he is not going to deter me from my purpose so he should just move on. I haven't forgotten the financial things that have been stolen from me either. So, I am also sure to remind him if he steals financially from me that I am keeping a tally including the interest of how much he will pay me back.

> *For God has not given us a spirit of fear, but of power and of love and of a sound mind* (2 Timothy 1:7 NKJV).

It took a lifetime to discover that I'd had my identity stolen by an enemy I could not see. We have a living Savior who has our back. We have a special purpose that God created particularly for us, not just corporately but each one of us as individuals. You have a purpose!

The devil is a liar. God loves you and the devil is lying because misery loves company. He simply wants to destroy you by convincing you that you are something you are not. The important thing to remember is that you are who God says you are—nothing less, nothing wanting. Satan hates your purpose and all it represents.

We have spiritual superpowers that we have not even begun to tap into. You see, God thinks our identity is important. When He made the world, He made Adam and Eve and He named them. He made them in His image and with His characteristics. The angels were in awe of man, they said, "Who is man that God is mindful of him?" (Psalm 8:4). So, that means that the angels are in awe of you and me. In the Garden of Eden, God gave man a choice, to choose provision and eternal life or to choose the tree of the knowledge of good, evil, and death. We have that choice again through Jesus Christ, so choose life.

God could have created us without a choice, but then we would not be His children. We would have been pets. It was interesting to me that the first thing God did after He made

Adam was to have him name what was in his authority. There is no other creature in the world like man.

The whole world was spoken into existence. You and I are made in the image of God, the children of the King, each one of us is a Prince or a Princess. I was born into privilege just like Adam and Eve. Adam and Eve gave away their birthright and gave the keys to the world to Satan who had already been thrown out of heaven for being the world's first identity thief. He wanted to be God and he tried to steal God's glory. He was so deceptive that he convinced one-third of the angels to go with him. However, that means Satan's demons are outnumbered two to one!

We are made in the image of God. When God was asked His name, He said, "I Am." God has been called many names that describe His nature, but when He was directly asked what His name was, He said, "I AM", which is the present tense. He did not say I was or I will. He is an ever-present God. We are not to live in the past but in the present. Every day say, "I Am ……." and fill in the blank with who God says you are!

God is the Alpha and the Omega. He is all-knowing. He is like a chess player, thinking millions of plays ahead. Always knowing the decisions and trouble we might get ourselves into,

He is waiting for us to call on His help. He is a great Father. He gave us the right to make decisions about our life. No matter what decision we make, good or bad, He is always there for us. He'll celebrate our good decisions and good consequences. He's there with open arms when we make wrong decisions and face bad consequences. I died and I still won. We have unmerited favor; we have grace because we can trust that He is a just and merciful God who keeps His promises and loves us.

> *And we know that all things work together for good to those who love God; to those who are the called according to His purposes* (Romans 8:28 NKJV).

It wasn't until I came to the end of what I could accomplish and asked God to drive my life that things started moving in the right direction.

He gave us the Bible, His Word as the framework, and infrastructure to the plan. He gave us countless examples of His will for healing and victories despite the mistakes we have made.

God said prosper. He said you will prosper as your soul prospers. How does your soul prosper? Your soul prospers by knowing God is number one in your life, understanding that He is not upset with you, and He has not caused any of the bad things in your life. He does not give you burdens to bear. He lifts the burdens that you were born into. We are all born into a lost world ruled by Satan. Jesus brought the Good News saying the Kingdom of Heaven is at hand. He is a loving God that has given us health, happiness, peace, provision, and complete communion with Him through His Son, Jesus Christ.

How do we make the giant leap from hoping for something, to working for something, and thinking we can get it through our plan and efforts? It is so simple that most people find it hard to grasp. It is done by believing that it's coming simply because God said it is ours.

When Jesus was in the desert with the devil, He had fasted for forty days. He was raised in the scriptures. He knew who He was. This is how it went...

> *Then Jesus was led by the Holy Spirit into the wilderness to be tempted by the devil. After He had gone without food for forty days and forty nights, He became hungry. The tempter came and said to Him, "If You are the Son of God, command that these stones to become bread." But Jesus replied,*

"It is written and forever remains written, 'Man shall not live by bread alone, but by every word that comes out of the mouth of God." Then the devil took Him into the holy city [Jerusalem] and placed Him on the pinnacle (highest point) of the temple. He said [mockingly] to Him, "If You are the Son of God, throw Yourself down; for it is written, 'He will command His angels concerning You [to serve, care for, protect and watch over You]'; and 'They will lift you on their hands, so that you will not strike your foot against a stone.'" Jesus said to him, "On the other hand, it is written and forever remains written, 'you shall not test the Lord your God.'"

Again, the devil took Him up on a very high mountain and showed Him all the kingdoms of the world and the glorious splendor, magnificence, and excellence of them; and he said to Him, "All these things I will give You if You fall and worship me." Then Jesus said to him, "Go away, Satan! For it is written and forever remains written, 'you shall worship the Lord your God, and serve Him

> *only.'" Then the devil left Him, and angels came and ministered to Him [bringing Him food and serving Him]* (Matthew 4:1-11 AMP).

Jesus knew that we were going to need more than the title of being a Christian. We were going to have to understand the warfare that came with it. We fight not against flesh and blood, but against spiritual beings in high places. He knew we would need full spiritual armor.

> *In conclusion, be strong in the Lord, draw your strength from Him and be empowered through your union with Him, and in the power of His boundless might. Put on the full armor of God for His precepts are like the splendid armor of a heavily-armed soldier, so that you may be able to successfully stand up against all the schemes and the strategies and the deceits of the devil. For our struggle is not against flesh and blood contending only with physical opponents, but against the rulers, against the powers, against the world forces of this present darkness, against the spiritual forces of wickedness in the heavenly supernatural places.*

> *Therefore, put on the full armor of God, so that you will be able to successfully resist and stand your ground in the evil day of danger, and having done everything that the crisis demands, to stand firm in your place, fully prepared, immovable, victorious]. So stand firm and hold your ground, having tightened the wide band of truth personal integrity, moral courage around your waist and having put on the breastplate of righteousness and upright heart, and having strapped on your feet the gospel of peace in preparation to face the enemy with firm-footed stability and the readiness produced by the good news. Above all, lift the protective shield of faith with which you can extinguish all the flaming arrows of the evil one. And take the helmet of salvation, and the sword of the Spirit, which is the Word of God* (Ephesians 6:10-17 AMP).

He knew we would need a weapon.

> *For the word of God is living and active and full of power [making it operative, energizing,*

> *and effective]. It is sharper than any two-edged sword, penetrating as fast as the division of his soul and spirit [the completeness of a person], and both joints and marrow [the deepest parts of our nature], exposing and judging the very thoughts and intentions of the heart* (Hebrews 4:12 AMP).

He said we we're not of this world. Jesus said, "They are not of the world, just as I am not of the world" (John 17:16 AMP).

> *Beloved, I urge you as aliens and strangers [in this world] to abstain from the sensual urges [those dishonorable desires] that wage war against the soul* (1 Peter 2:11 AMP).

> *When Jesus was asked how to pray he said: Pray, then, in this way:*

> *'Our Father who is in heaven, Hallowed be Your name. Your kingdom come, Your will be done on earth as it is in heaven. Give us this day our daily bread. And forgive us our debts, as we have forgiven our debtors [letting go of both the*

> *wrong and resentment]. And do not lead us into temptation but deliver us from evil. [For Yours is the kingdom and the power, and the glory forever. Amen]* (Matthew 6:9-13 AMP).

He said behold the Kingdom of Heaven is at hand. We must understand that we have the laws from the Kingdom of Heaven that we are adopted into versus the laws of this worldly kingdom. We must choose to go by the laws of this world or the laws of the Kingdom of Heaven. Where are those laws? There are over 3,000 of them in the Bible that work on our behalf. They are the promises of God and they do not return void. They go out like arrows seeking a target and they never miss.

However, if you don't know them you can't speak to them. The spoken word is more powerful than the written word. It is one thing to recite scriptures, it's another thing to know deep down in your spirit that the word is true and be able to say it knowing that you are making a heavenly declaration that cannot fail. You know that if it came from your father, the King and Creator of the universe, it is the most powerful decree of all. Unfortunately, so many of us do not know who we are or whose we are. We are living in an identity crisis.

Stolen identity is like waking up with amnesia. Imagine

waking up one day and you know your name, but you are in a house that you are not sure is yours. You have clothes in the closet that you are not sure how they got there. You have a car, but you are not sure where you are supposed to go with it. There is money, food, and everything else that you need, but you do not know where it all came from. This is a literal picture of how it felt for me before I died and how knowing my identity felt after I died and came back.

Suddenly, I went from being a Christian with a title, to a Christian with a purpose and a mission. Before I had the helmet of protection and the armor of God, now I not only knew my weapons and my mission, but I also had everything I would ever need to accomplish what God called me to do. I could have total access to the plan. I just had to wait for it. You see the plan can change. It changes based on how I move the pieces on the chessboard. The decisions I make are still mine to make and they still have consequences.

So, the secret to living a God-led life is to be led by God in your decision making. This takes effort, it takes discipline, and attaining the knowledge that this is not a game. It is real. Heaven is real, God is real, the consequences are real, and the enemy is real. The plan is like a maze where you know eventually you will get out. You must ask someone with a different perspective than you, who is looking down on the situation and can tell you if you should go left or right. That someone is Jesus of course.

Now let us add to the maze a real enemy, some of your lapses in judgment, and a few wrong decisions into the mix. I can tell you that you need to know the rules of engagement. You need to know what the Word of God says about you and who is with you in the battle. I know God, I know the Holy Spirit, and I speak in tongues. I have always called it my prayer language and used it for powerful prayer time with God and intercession. One day, I read in 1 Corinthians these words:

> *Though I speak with the tongues of men and angels but have not love, I have become sounding brass or a clanging cymbal. And though I have the gift of prophecy, and understand all mysteries and all knowledge, and though I have all faith, so that I could remove mountains, but have not love, I am nothing. And though I bestow all my goods to feed the poor, and though I give my body to be burned, but have not love, it profits me nothing.*

> *Love suffers long and is kind; love does not envy; love does not parade itself, is not puffed up; does not behave rudely, does not seek its own, is not provoked, thinks no evil; does not rejoice in iniquity, but rejoices with the truth; bears all things, believes all things, hopes all things, endures all things. Love never fails. But whether there are prophecies, they will fail; whether there are tongues, they will cease; whether there is knowledge, it will vanish away.... And now abide faith, hope, love, these three; but the greatest of these is love* (1 Corinthians 13:1-8, 13 NKJV).

It was the first time I put it together that I had God the Father as my King, Jesus as my advocate, the Holy Spirit as my comforter, and two angels on my side for every demon in hell that would come up against me. I spoke their language. However, none of this would be as important to my mission on this planet as having love. Love is the language that transcends all languages.

This was the first time I also realized that God is all of these things! The Bible says that God is love, and if you replace the word love with God in this passage, you can know the nature of your Heavenly Father. I realized that God is not mad at me! When I make mistakes, when I make wrong decisions, when I am willful, rebellious, and foolish, He still loves me and accepts me!

I started living a life of expectation without fear of death or failure. I used to go into a battle wondering if I could win. Now, I go in knowing that with God I cannot lose. I also know that if I get too obsessed with what I can do instead of what God has done, I will trip myself up. Do I have this all figured out? No, I have to renew my mind every day to remember who I am. It's like going to a mirror and seeing myself for the first time every day.

I have four enemies, the devil, his demons, distractions of life, and my own thoughts not aligned with God's Word. They all can be defeated with faith that the Word of God is true, His kingdom is real, and that you and I are real citizens in His Kingdom. However, faith without works is dead. Therefore, I must always know and be about the purpose that God has given me. You are probably wondering if that means author, teacher, preacher, and business owner. No, it means to love.

> *Jesus answered, "The first and most important (commandment) is: 'Hear O Israel, The Lord our*

> *God is one Lord; and you shall love the Lord your God with all your heart, and with all your soul (life), and with all your mind (thought, understanding), and with all your strength.' This is the second: 'you shall [unselfishly] love your neighbor as yourself." There is no other commandment greater than these* (Mark 12:29-31 AMP).

Unfortunately, if the devil has stolen your identity, you don't love yourself. You need to understand that you are more than the sum of the physical body that you are in, the money in your bank account, the recognition of your peers and loved ones, the gifts you received, or your legacy. You are an alien to this world on a spiritual mission to love God's children back into the kingdom. God loved you enough to send His only Son to come for you to have a choice.

> *For God so [greatly] loved and dearly prized the world, that He [even] gave His [One and] only begotten Son, so that whoever believes and trusts in Him [as Savior] shall not perish but have eternal life. For God did not send the Son into the world to judge and condemn the world [that is,*

> *to initiate the final judgment of the world], but that the world might be saved through Him* (John 3:16-17 AMP).

After I died and experienced the love of God firsthand. I was taught all these lessons that I learned, I have moments of snapping my fingers and saying to the Devil, "I Am a Child of the King and have the power in the name above all names, the name of Jesus Christ." I have watched the devil vanish in my circumstances.

God is the author and finisher of our faith. Faith must be set free; you must make the decisions to let God turn the impossible into it's possible. You see, the Bible says that if you have faith like a mustard seed, the tiniest of seeds by the way, you will grow the biggest tree in the garden. In another scripture, it says that each one of us has been given the measure of faith. This means you have a faith bank account, and it already has faith in it to move mountains. How do you earn more faith to put in that bank account?

> *Faith comes by hearing the word of God. So then faith comes by hearing and hearing by the word of God* (Romans 10:17 AMP).

You can keep growing your faith through hearing the Word of God, hearing the testimonies of the saints, and being fully convinced that this invisible currency is real. However, God did not bankroll you with faith for just you. He wanted you to have compassion for your brothers and sisters and bring them into the Kingdom of Heaven so they can have all their needs met in this world and the next.

Jesus is our example. That is the truth of who God is. That little thing called compassion that makes us human is the characteristic that says louder than anything, "I am my father's child. I am willing to dedicate my life by giving my heart and loving people to fulfill a greater purpose of letting people know the love of God for them."

If we knew everything about His full purpose and plan for our lives, we may not be able to handle it with our current level of understanding, belief, and faith. If our current identity, understanding, belief, and faith are wrong because of an identity crisis, we do not know who we are. God gives us one step at a time, growing us along the path of our destiny to eventually fulfill His grand plan for our lives for the greater purpose.

Now write out your declaration of who you are as God has told you through His written Word:

Your Declaration:

____

____

____

ELEVEN
IDENTITY THEFT: WHO I WAS BEFORE

To understand how far I have come, you must know where I came from. I came from being a miracle.

I was born four months too early on February 5th, 1968. I weighed 29 ounces at birth. I was born at 22 weeks of pregnancy, so my lungs were barely formed. Every time a doctor had a bad prognosis and said that I would not live, that I would have an intellectual disability, be blind or delayed in any way, my mother held on to her faith by searching for my name in a baby name book. She found the name Danielle, which meant "God is her Judge." She said to the doctors, "She will live. Her name is Danielle." Which meant to her that only God could decide my fate.

She said she recalled looking at me in the incubator and heard my voice in her mind saying, "Mommy, if you don't pray for me who will?" She knew that somebody had to have faith that I could be a miracle. You see, Jesus made up His mind when He went to the cross that I could live and not die.

> *I shall not die, but live, and declare the works of the Lord* (Psalm 118:17 KJV).

> *Even then God had designs on me. Why, when I was still in my mother's womb he chose and called me out of sheer generosity! (Galatians 1:15, MSG)*

How do I explain my life before I died? I was 48 when I died. The most positive things about my life were that I had five children and an awesome husband. My life was calming down. Unfortunately, I had a lot of broken identity before then. I was born at 5 months 2 weeks, one of three living children, from different wives. My mother was my dad's third wife. My father had gone through three marriages and had buried 27 children due to miscarriages when I was born. My mother already had at least five pregnancies, all born too early. She would have ten pregnancies. I ended up being the only child she had that survived. All her miscarriages happened at about five months of term.

To my family, I was a miracle child. My mother said on the day I was born my birth certificate was issued, that they started early on my death certificate based on their prior experiences. They also moved her off the maternity ward in order to spare her the pain of watching other parents leave the hospital with their healthy children. Despite little hope, my mother had decided in her heart to pray for a miracle and to believe the unbelievable. She thought "only God can decide if she lives or dies." She went down to the incubator to look at my tiny body, which had no fat on it. I looked at her like a tiny rat, my eyes bandaged and tubes running from everywhere. She said she heard a voice in her head say, "Mommy, if you won't pray for me who will?" She went to the yellow pages and started calling every church in Lake Charles to pray: Catholic, Baptist, Full Gospel, it did not matter. She just asked them all to pray. Well God heard them, and I beat all the odds.

In 1968, the chances were probably slim to none of my survival. Except with God, who decided that I would end up with no serious problems at all. The newspapers followed the story and did an article on it. I even made the local papers.

American Press 1912 - 2002, Thursday, March 14, 1968, Page: 25

'Two-pound bundle' is hospital's joy

Danielle Thibodeaux is only 39 days old today but she has become the sweetheart of all who see her in her tiny sleeping niche at Lake Charles Memorial Hospital.

Danielle, which means God is my judge, was one pound 13 ounces when she was born at 9 a.m. Feb. 7.

Wednesday afternoon she moved upwards to the "heavy-weight" division having added nearly seven ounces since birth.

Her parents, Mr. and Mrs. Clarence Thibodeaux of 1305 13th St. are elated over the steady progress the tiny girl is making.

"She kicked so much when when she was born we thought they would have to tie her down with sand bags," Mrs. Thibodeaux, the former Jeanny Lambright of Oberlin said.

"We will bring her home when she weighs five pounds," the mother said. Thibodeaux, a division manager for Citizens Standard Life Insurance Co. said "she's a wonderful baby —with so much energy."

Danielle's tiny quarters today is an incubator and the parents get to see her regularly. Everyone keeps an eye on the squirming, kicking infant. She was born prematurely at five and a half months.

I Was One in a Million

The story that I was a miracle, would be my defining memory as a child growing up. Almost immediately in life, the enemy came to rob me of that title. I was molested as a child and a teenager on different occasions and by different people. My parents had no idea what was happening to me. My parents were busy with careers and a volatile marriage, alcohol was not their friend and it usually led them down the wrong path into knockdown, drag-out fights. They were super professionals and lived what I thought was a normal life during the day except for these late-night episodes that became more and more frequent.

I had two half-siblings from my father's prior marriages. My brother 25 years older than me was already grown and had children of his own and my sister, was 10 years older.

My sister and I were raised in the same house. She acted as my protector. She would shield me from as much drama going on in my home as she could. She often took on a lot more responsibility than she should've had to. She was smart and moved out when she was 17. From that point on, I had to deal with the full brunt of my parents fighting and drinking on my own. I had issues at the time that no one was aware of because I had been molested by a babysitter's son, who would end up killing himself. This would not be the last time something bad happened to me of this nature.

My parents got divorced when I was about eight. It was terrible. Both my parents were accusing each other of having affairs and both did have relationships right away with people they worked with. My mom got custody of me; she was an apartment manager who helped investors flip big apartment complexes. This meant we moved constantly into bad areas. She often had to evict and fire people all at the same time, so it was not unusual for us to be threatened with harm and hated. She would move police officers onto the properties and move them around us to protect us. Our life was volatile and stressful, sometimes dangerous.

My Saving Grace

My saving grace during these years was my belief in God. It was my salvation. I had gotten saved at 11 and I would come to depend on God more than my parents. At about age 13, I would end up at a place called Happy Church, with Marylyn Hickey and her husband, Wally Hickey and their daughter Sara. They had a great influence on my faith and understanding of how God worked. I remember Marylyn Hickey coming up to the youth group and praying and prophesying over each one of us. When she prayed, she said I would be Deborah, a woman in the bible that led God's people. The idea that I would become anything or that God had any plans for me started there and the prayer sparked hope in me, that I have not forgotten till this day.

My mother had a volatile job flipping apartment complexes, that kept us in constant chaos. Unfortunately, we moved so much I could not keep track of the schools I went to; I only know that I went to seven different High Schools. My dad lived with his secretary who he eventually married. My mom married her alcoholic maintenance man. He was a violent drunk and was abusive to me. Sometimes I would come home to him sitting in the dark drinking, looking scary, and waiting for a fight. My mother ended up meeting someone else, so she divorced him and moved on. My mom went on a binge of dating broken men and trying to fix them in the name of Jesus, all while she was living a double life as an alcoholic abuser herself. I called it dating evangelism.

She finally went for help for her alcoholism, but unfortunately she was not cured from the dating evangelism. She met a man in alcoholics anonymous named Larry. She was drawn to the fact that he had been a sponsor and fancied himself to become a minister. He was an ex-con from Detroit, who had been in prison for armed robbery and heroin addiction. Immediately after he left living in a half-way house, he moved in with us and he started drinking again. He was abusive mentally and physically in every way possible to her and to me. She was always believing for the man to become a preacher. So, I now say my mother has great faith. Unfortunately, no matter how much you want for someone to change their life for the better, or you want them to follow God, it can't happen without their permission. Lesson One: People must be willing to work with God; they have free will. She would pick the ones that needed the most help and try to save them without their willingness to submit their lives to God.

I would end up going back and forth between my parents never feeling settled. My mom's abusive husband was someone to get away from. My father's wife made it clear that I was a burden. In my junior year of high school, my mother and I were beaten so badly by Larry over a number of days that I ended up in the emergency room and my mother had literally gone out of her mind. I overheard them talking about their being only one space left in the battered women's shelter. I was in high school and was only 17, they explained the situation and I bowed out and said I was 18 so they offered to send her to a battered women's shelter. I sent her off and let them believe I was older and didn't need the help. She ended up in a battered women's shelter fifty miles away. I was just about to turn 18 and I ended up homeless for a season. I had learned a lot of lessons about depending on God during that season.

Homeless but Not Helpless

During my time of being homeless, I lived in an abandoned house, attended school and church, and did odd jobs in the area. I focused on survival. I would keep food at the local store because I had no electricity. The owner let me get what I had stored there every day. It was my desire to get out of that house to somewhere safer and to finish High School, so I was praying for a way that could happen. Sometimes I didn't sleep in the house because the doors of the house were warped and would not close. There was no plumbing either. Drug dealers were in the area. Afraid of getting raped, I would sometimes lock myself into a baseball dugout and sleep on the bench. School was where I ate and showered. On the weekends church was the place to go, there were people and I felt safe. No one knew why I would go up and sob at the altar. I was happy that my mom was safe and that she was not being hurt anymore. I hoped her mind would come back. I hadn't heard from her. She was in a season where she could not contact outsiders.

One day, I passed by a payphone outside the grocery store, and it rang, I thought why not, and answered it for fun.

To my surprise, the woman on the other end of the line asked, "Is Danielle there?" I said, "I am Danielle, how did you know I was here?"

She said they had called earlier, someone had answered the phone and said that I would be there in an hour. I had no set time to go to the store or to pass this phone booth. I was stunned, to say the least.

At a loss for an explanation, I asked the woman what she needed. She said she was looking for someone to work children's ministry at the church. I had never called the church or left a number for them to call me. I asked her how she got this number, she said that I was in her heart and low and behold she looked down and saw my name written on a pad next to the phone number. I saw this as a sign to say yes!

I told her I was interested and gave her the address of the store. She said she would pick me up there on Sunday morning. This was totally a phone booth miracle.

That Sunday, I went and waited for the lady to pick me up for church to work as a helper in her children's ministry. To my surprise, the police showed up to ask me questions. The grocery store owner was concerned about me, a young girl living on the streets, and had decided to intervene. Just as I was trying to answer questions about my situation, the woman from the children's ministry pulled up in a van. A well-dressed, tall, blond-haired woman stepped out of the van, and came over and very calmly began to speak to the police on my behalf.

When they asked where I lived, she said, "She lives with me."

Just like that, I had a home with a former missionary family from Uganda. She helped me get a job. Then she helped find foster care for me in spite of my age, my next place to live, and she got me back in touch with my father. He said I could come and live with him and finish school. He came to get me to go to school in my senior year.

Looking for Love in all the Wrong Places

Consequently, my youth did not leave me with much self-esteem. So, when a man came along and said he loved me, I believed him. He was a Marine named Mark, who was headed for Iraq. He wanted to get married before he left for Desert Shield, so we got married after only three short months of knowing each other. The truth about the relationship that drove me into it so fast was that I fell in love with "normal." His family took pictures for no reason, baked cookies together, and had family events. I wanted that, I wanted to belong.

I overlooked his problems. He was gone on military events that would forever change him for most of our five-year marriage. He would end up cheating on me blatantly and repeatedly. He was exposed and then addicted to pornography, and he got deeper and deeper into it. This drove a wedge between us, and we became more and more distant. However, I was determined to make it work because of my faith and my children. We had two daughters together, Gabrielle and Amanda.

I stayed around and ended up eating my pain. After a pregnancy on bed rest with lots of complications and feeling rejected and lost in my marriage, I ended up weighing 300 pounds. I was a military wife alone with a baby on a military base far away from anyone I knew. I blamed myself for everything that was going wrong in our marriage. My self-esteem, as low as it was plummeted even more. The more he was cheating and looking at pornography, the more I saw my reflection as the problem of our marriage. No matter how wrong he was for cheating and beating me up, I blamed myself. I was sure he was openly sickened by me as he often pointed to other women and compared them to me. Once he turned us around at the door of a party because he could not stand to be seen with me. He went to training for 6 months and I decided that I would try to change my appearance to please him.

I got weight loss surgery and lost 100 pounds and we took one more try at it. He still cheated despite my new appearance. We got divorced after Desert Shield, when I was still pregnant with my second daughter, Amanda. He still visited with the girls, but his life got more and more strange. He had an addiction to pornography, and he lived outside the lines more and more with his lifestyle. At one point, he was living with two women and having a relationship back and forth with both of them playing them against each other. The court gave him strict guidelines about who he could introduce to our daughter Gabrielle, but he still had visitation with her and her younger sister, Amanda.

One day, my daughter Gabrielle started acting strangely. I brought her to the pediatrician and to make a long investigation short, to my horror, I found out she was molested. Through investigation, it came out in her therapy that the culprit was her own father. I pressed charges and we went through years of investigation, courtroom battles, and therapy sessions. Mark would get out of the initial criminal charges by having his girlfriend break my nose on that day of court, so I wouldn't show up to testify.

Many balls were dropped that day and his case was dismissed for lack of witnesses and evidence. Still, the evidence was overwhelming enough to remove his rights in family court concerning our older daughter. However, in Louisiana every child is separate, so he had a right to go for custody of the other child.

With the criminal trial behind him, he decided to go for custody of our second daughter, Amanda the one he had not been around as much. I would end up having two different lawyers after the older one died of a heart attack during my case. The younger one died shortly thereafter in a car crash before he ever made it to court.

To make matters worse, right in the middle of my court battle, I got a new neighbor. An ex-con moved in across the street from my house with his blind grandmother. I did not know anything about him at the time, only that she was blind and needed his help. He came to the house one night under the guides of borrowing a can opener. I did not know about his past. I opened the door, and he came in and raped me. Afraid of bringing negative attention to myself and fear that I would have a stigma, I went to the hospital, got a rape kit, and hid it from the world.

I was crushed inside, but I was continuing to go to church at the time and told myself that God would use the experience to help me help other women one day. It was also during this season my father was diagnosed with terminal cancer. He had been my only support system. He had provided me with a home, did homework with my daughter, and picked them up after school while I worked. He died before the end of my court case. Devastated by my circumstances, out of money and hope, living out of a battered women's shelter for a time, and then taking women home with me who had no place to go, my house on Mandy Street was lovingly called the Mandy Street Mission.

I was determined to turn anything bad around for good. I went back to school at night to become a paralegal to fight my own case. I fought the case myself for four years and with God's help through a dream that would help me recognize a legal theory, I ended up changing the law in Louisiana. One day, I caught the eye of a young lawyer by the name of Kevin, who saw me struggle in court one day, came up behind me and whispered some legal advice. I was constantly asking the Judge for what attorneys call sidebars or private meetings. The Judge would accept because I was a tongue-tied novice representing myself. I did not know what I was saying or asking for half of the time, only what I needed to happen. That day the Judge, seeing an opportunity, called Kevin out and told him that I would be his new pro bono client. Kevin graciously accepted seeing his own case was up next and he hoped for favor from the Judge.

Kevin gave me free advice and we became good friends and then we became more. After some convincing I agreed to date him. I initially said no, not because I didn't like him, but because I did not think I was worthy of him. Nevertheless, my relationship with Kevin got serious and I began to help him open his own law firm. We were a great legal team. I accepted that his family would not sign off on the relationship. We worked in the law firm together and professionally were a great match. This was as close as I had ever come to normal, so I ignored that spiritually we were on different levels. I was out on Bourbon Street witnessing to folks and he was content to go to mass on holidays only.

He proposed marriage, but his family did not like that I had a sketchy past and that I was not Catholic. We attempted to go to the altar at least five times over our eight-year relationship. He would make excuses and a few times left me at the altar, like the runaway groom. I was determined that I was going to live by Christian values, so during the entire relationship, we never had sex. I was determined to do things the right way. I believed it was because of respect that he never challenged me on it, always respecting my wishes.

I should have questioned that our relationship was not moving forward at a normal pace, but I wanted to believe the best. I wanted more children and was eager to get married. I held on to hope and kept pushing him. He was a smart, dry-witted, super-intelligent, high-functioning alcoholic, and I ignored the alcohol part. Instead, I watered down his drinks and told myself he did not have a problem because he was not mean. I too was practicing dating evangelism.

We tried counseling. Despite the counselor telling me to walk away, I had such low self-esteem that I kept trying. After all, I had married an abusive child molester, so a skittish, high-functioning alcoholic lawyer who treated me well for the most part, seemed like an improvement.

Then, Hurricane Katrina came along and ripped me out of New Orleans and out of the relationship altogether. I ended up in Houston, Texas with my two daughters in their preteens. My relationship with Kevin persisted over the phone and through visits. We still planned to get married. In my mind, there was still hope because he could leave New Orleans and start a new life with me. I had even lined up a job for him in Texas. I just could not let go of the idea of forcing it to work. Eight years of waiting was a huge down payment on the future that I had dreamed of.

I think if God could have put both hands on my shoulders and shook me and said give up, I have a plan for you, it would have been as big a shake as Hurricane Katrina. However, no matter what the Holy Spirit was telling me I stayed in New Orleans. It took Hurricane Katrina ripping me out of New Orleans altogether. However, it was not without warning. Just before the hurricane, I had a dream of a storm where God told me I should not be afraid of the storm, that He was wiping my slate clean and moving me on to build a new life. Did I use the opportunity to call it quits, NO. I still did it my way and had a long-distance relationship, until one day I went to a cartoon conference for my kids in the middle of Houston. Who should

I run into but, Kevin! He was there with another woman and her kids on a family outing in Houston, only months after Katrina. I knew the woman, she was our receptionist at the law firm. It was not a coincidence. Houston has 4 million people in it, and God was ready for me to wake up. Kevin was with the receptionist that I had hired. It turned out he had been having an affair with her for quite some time.

Now the cat was out of the bag. My heart was crushed, but I was free to move on. I left being a paralegal behind me. I went back to work as a cosmetologist in hair replacement. My mother, now a widow had also come with me to Houston. I ended up moving to Clear Lake City, a suburb south of Houston. I will never forget walking into my new apartment after I had found out about Kevin's betrayal.

My mother said, "You are here because your future husband is here."

This was a bold statement after all I had just been through, but she was right. My husband was there.

However, it was not the last time I would hear from Kevin. He kept in touch and often called me about cases and to talk to the girls. After all I had been through with him in my life, I did not want my girls to have one more drama to go through, so we opted to remain friends. Deep down, I had not forgiven him for the eight-year relationship and the lies, but my girls were attached. I treated the end of the relationship like an amicable divorce. Surprisingly, he married the receptionist not long after.

After a while, I settled into my new life and became very successful with my job. I started to have a social life and had some money in the bank. I bought a car on my own and was starting to lose weight and worry about my appearance. I joined Amway to sell cosmetics and vitamins outside of my regular job.

The key moment in my development of me was me saying, "Lord, if it is just, You and me and my kids, then I am good. You are all I need."

My husband Jim talks about being in the exact same place in his life. It was in Amway that I met one of the leaders, my future husband Jim Royce. Although we knew each other in business, our kids had made friends at school, bringing us together outside of the business. My birthday rolled around, he found out that we shared the birthday month, and our birthdays were only one day apart. We went on our first date on my birthday, stayed up talking past midnight, and ended on his birthday. We hit it off so well and were so in tune that night that the food got cold sitting on the table and we never ate it. Meeting Jim was like finding a missing part of me that I didn't know existed yet. There was no doubt that night that I had a soulmate, and he was sitting across the table from me. The great thing was he knew it at the same time I did. The first thing we fell in love with about each other was how much we both loved the Lord. Our relationship was everything I could have ever dreamed of. Jim was and is an amazing friend, husband, father, and on fire for God! I knew without a doubt that I had met the one God had for me.

Jim and I went on to date for a year and I had concluded that I had found my soulmate. Kevin kept in touch with the girls and I and I believed him to be happy. At least that is the story Kevin told me. My girls thought of him as a father because he had been there acting like one for eight years. Jim and I announced our engagement, and we were excited to plan our future together. Just when I thought that everything was working out as it was meant to be, Kevin's tune changed just after I announced I was getting married to Jim. He made excuses to call on cases and to talk to the girls, but it was clear that he was upset. He started to be open about his doubts about his recent marriage, calling me out of the blue to complain about his choices. Only I had no doubts about Jim. I asked him to only call and talk to the girls, but the closer it got to my wedding date the more he called. I wasn't picking up anymore. Then I hit a snag. I tried to get the documents from the New Orleans Courthouse to get married to Jim and they couldn't find them. Kevin and I had attempted to get married prior and we obtained the necessary documentation to do so, and Kevin had the only certified copy in his filing cabinet. The category five storm had wiped out the documents that would allow me to marry. Our usually friendly conversations became more and more strained. I was asking for my paperwork from my prior divorce and my birth certificate, all of which were underwater in the archives of New Orleans and only existed in his third-floor office. He would make excuses about not being able to find the paperwork despite me having a visual memory and telling which file drawer it was in.

It became clear that he wanted to have his cake and eat it too. I told him it was unfair for him to cheat on me, get married, and expect me to have no life forever. It took him a minute to realize it, but he knew I was right. I guess it never occurred to him how he would feel when it was my turn to be happy. Unfortunately, his married life was not all that he had imagined at the time, so this did not help matters or ease his doubts that he had made a mistake. On the other hand, I was sure about my relationship with Jim. Jim proposed and I accepted. Jim wanted me to know that he was all in, so he bought a house before we ever got married and moved us all in it. He moved in with his parents while waiting for our wedding day. I had one big problem; Kevin had not given me my paperwork and he had the only copy.

This is It

Kevin had a certified copy of my former divorce papers from my ex-husband. We had gotten it for our attempts down the aisle. We had needed them for our wedding. I kept asking him to mail them to me, and he would say he did, or he would backtrack and say he forgot. Finally, I called his bluff and said I was coming to Louisiana to pick them up in person. He came clean and said that he knew it was not fair and he had regrets, but he was not going to sabotage me getting married and being happy. He would say everything I wanted to hear but he was stalling in lawyerly fashion. My wedding was only two weeks away and I was beginning to panic, so I planned a trip to Louisiana.

I remember telling him, "You got married, you're happy, why can't I be happy too?"

He finally came to his senses and agreed to cooperate with me. He said he knew it was irrational, but he felt that this was it. Our friendship would be over. I said that I hoped he would stay in touch with the girls. He asked to speak to my girls and told them that they were to obey me, be good to their new stepdad, and that if they ever needed him, he would be there for them.

He told me, "You know I will love you until I die."

I said I loved him, too. After all he had been with me through so much. He had been my best friend for eight years and had gotten me through hell and back. I said that I would never forget all that he had done for me and my girls and that he was instrumental in my life. I would not have made it through everything without him. The truth was our friendship was bigger than our relationship.

When he called me back later with the tracking number for the papers, he said one thing I will never forget, "Write this tracking number down. This is the only copy, and I will not be able to do this again."

I repeated the tracking number back to him and we said

goodbye at about four o'clock in the afternoon. The next morning, I got a phone call from his number at 9 a.m. I almost didn't pick up, angrily thinking that we had just said he was going to stop calling every day and making excuses. I picked up the phone anyway thinking that it might have something to do with the papers and another excuse.

To my surprise, I heard a woman talking to me on the other side of the phone. It was his wife, Rene. I could tell from the tone in her voice that she was shocked that I was the one to pick up the phone. I quickly prepared myself mentally for a conversation explaining that I was getting married and that I had only talked to Kevin to get the paperwork.

She paused for a moment and said in a matter-of-fact voice, "Kevin is dead."

I exclaimed, "What?!"

A huge knot formed in my throat, and I could not breathe for a moment.

I summoned up all the courage I could, and hoping this was a cruel joke asked, "How did he die? Did he get into an accident; did you let him drink and drive?"

She said, "He drank eight bottles of vodka last night and died in his sleep."

She said she wanted to know who he had talked to last, so she dialed the last phone number.

Weeping and trying to catch my breath, I said, "Okay, I must tell the kids."

I hung up the phone and lost it. I was at my new job in the breakroom. I slumped down to a chair. Sobbing uncontrollably, I drew everyone's attention in the place. In my mind, Satan himself was loading me up with overwhelming guilt and condemnation. At the time, I was thinking that I had something to do with his state of mind. I kept thinking about how I never told her to water down his drinks; I never told her he was an alcoholic at all. Ridiculously, I blamed myself. I felt as though she didn't have the full instructions for keeping Kevin alive the way I had for so many years.

Looking back, it was ridiculous for me to take responsibility for his death. Nevertheless, I did. I called Jim, and he met me at the house to tell my daughters the terrible inexplicable news of how he died. Almost on cue, we were interrupted by a knock at the door with the FedEx package at noon that day. Nothing was in the package but the legal paperwork. I kept hoping it was a cruel prank and I would find the punch line in the envelope. Jim and I were supposed to get married in two weeks, so I washed my face, and in a few short days, we all packed for a wedding, and a funeral.

Since Hurricane Katrina, people had been disconnected, and no one in New Orleans was communicating much, so they still thought Kevin and I were married. We had been telling everyone we were married ever since the first time he left me at the altar to save the explanation and embarrassment. So, I kept getting the condolences that were meant for a wife. Some of his family would not talk to me, and his law partner straight out said I was the reason for his death. For the people who did not know as much, it was a difficult time trying to point them in the direction of his new wife and catch them up on life after Katrina. I also had Jim standing there with me and introduced him as my fiancé.

I'll never forget some guy with a big Texas accent saying, "Why you're just burying them and marrying them ain't ya!"

It was horrible. I could not wait to leave. I quietly walked over to his body and said goodbye. His wife was sitting alone on one side of the funeral home and the family was sitting on the other side. Evidently, she was not what they had in mind either. They had already started threatening her to sign over the law firm. I could not hold a grudge against her. I saw how she was being treated and thought this could have been me. So, to be kind, Jim and I sat with her and her kids at the funeral. No one in his family or his circles was giving her the time of day.

So, we went one step further and went home with her after the funeral, to keep her from being alone. She was hurt, angry, and in shock. She wanted me to see all their wedding pictures and toured me around the home, totally insensitive to how I might be upset over all the pictures and memories that started at least a year before I knew my relationship with Kevin was over. I was in a daze as she told me to my face how long they had been having a relationship behind my back.

I think, because of the shortness of her marriage, she needed to somehow prove that the relationship had been going on for some time. She was sort of living backward at this point. She even asked if she could have any old pictures of Kevin and me. When I asked why she would want them, she said so she could cut me out of the pictures. I was blown away at these moments that were actually happening and also torn with guilt, grief, anger, and betrayal. Every emotion was bombarding me at the same time.

Simultaneously, I was thankful this was not my life anymore. I could leave there and never look back. All of this happened at their kitchen table in their apartment. I deserved an academy award. I was the greatest actress in the world at this point.

I kindly excused myself and said, "Well, we hate to go, but we have plans."

I walked without any emotion into the parking lot. I remember Jim stopping me and firmly planting himself in my path in the parking lot as we left her house. He blocked me from moving forward and looked me in the eyes as if he had been having a conversation with himself the whole time.

He said in a firm voice, "Forget that! I am your fiancé, I love you! So, it's okay if you want to scream and yell at the top of your lungs, do it! I will understand. You do not have to fake it with me."

I hugged him, cried, and wished it had not happened. I wanted it to be a nightmare that I could wake up from. Jim held me and I cried. Then we went to pick up my daughters from seeing their half-sisters. My ex-husband had remarried and had two more daughters. He was separated from their mother, so I thought it was safe to say yes to the girls to go and see their half-sisters. I had not given any instruction to their mother about them not seeing my ex-husband. They were getting a divorce, and I did not imagine he would be around.

However, when I went in to get the girls, he was there. My

nightmare had just folded over onto itself and gotten worse. This was the monster I had fought against. My girls were in their teens now and could handle themselves. It seemed he had only been there for a short while. I asked my girls if they were okay, and they said yes. I watched as my ex-husband, Mark shook the hand of my fiancé, Jim, and introduced himself like a man talking about his old used car. I cannot remember what he said, but he made some reference to how my personality had been so he could prove that he had prior knowledge.

I wanted to scream, "Let me out! Let me out of this nightmare, somebody wake me up." I took solace in remembering a day prior to Katrina that I had dragged Kevin to the church to make him meet with a pastor. The pastor was not there that day, but an older gentleman was available, and he knew just how to talk to Kevin. He ended up praying with him to receive salvation that day. I could only hope that Kevin was in heaven.

Our Beautiful Wedding

The next day we took a tour of New Orleans for Jim to see it. Then, we left New Orleans and headed back to Houston, where we left our kids with family. We went alone to Colorado to get married at Victoria's Keep, a Victorian bed and breakfast. Arriving in Colorado was like stepping through a portal into another dimension. It looked like a postcard, the air was fresh, the sky was blue, and the past seemed a million miles behind us. Jim and I had a beautiful wedding that looked and felt like a complete fairytale. Although I was deeply saddened by Kevin's death. I knew in my heart that Kevin was with the Lord and that Satan had done everything he could to stop this wedding.

I remember feeling like I had stepped out of a nightmare into a fairy tale as I dressed for the wedding and headed down the steep stairwell to the front porch that overlooked the picturesque mountains and had a running stream not 20 feet in front of the porch. Behind the pale blue and white 1800 Victorian house surrounded by flowers there was an actual castle. We took gorgeous pictures. The honeymoon was amazing, we took long walks in the mountains and lost ourselves for a little while.

I remember turning the corner of the door of the bed and breakfast and heading onto the porch to see Jim and thinking, "No looking back, No turning back, I choose Happiness." After the honeymoon, we came back and had a reception with our family.

Brethren, I count not myself to have apprehended: but this one thing I do, forgetting those things which are behind, and reaching forth unto those things which are before, I press toward the mark for the prize of the high calling of God in Christ Jesus (Philippians 3:13-14).

Settling into Our New Life

We settled into our house in a good neighborhood and life moved on at an extremely fast pace. We quickly learned that single parenting had left our teens lacking some skills, so I homeschooled our four teens to get to know them and to sort of rein them in. This was not an easy choice, and a bold move since neither of us had ever done that before. We joined a small church. We both had experience with being children's workers and Jim had been a youth pastor, so we were quickly nominated to become the new children's pastors of the church.

I had just turned 40 and all of our kids were about to graduate from high school. With four proms and four cars and four cell phones outside of our own, we were fantasizing about extra money and free time.

After meeting Jim, I wanted to turn back time and live my life over again. Part of me wished that I had met Jim when I was younger so we could have children together. However, I knew it was probably never going to happen. I had endometriosis and low progesterone and had trouble getting pregnant when I was 23, so at 40, I figured it was not going to happen. We never even thought it could happen. God had different plans. At 40 years old, I found out I was pregnant with our son Michael.

I remember being so shocked about being pregnant, I went to the hospital to get an ultrasound to get proof of life before I ever spoke to Jim. It was a big thing, and Jim had even called me right in the middle of the whole thing. I lied to him for the first time. He caught it of course, and asked me to meet him for coffee to see what was up with me. I met Jim after and slid the picture across the table. We were shocked, excited, nervous, and thrilled all at the same time.

Michael was exactly the glue our little family needed to make it complete. The teenagers were now solidified as brothers and sisters, all because of the love of a little brother. We would call him Michael Josiah Royce. Michael for the archangel of course, Josiah because he was a boy-king of Israel who served God in the Bible, and our last name means Royalty. So, we considered him our Royal Angel King.

We had all the normal drama, and a little abnormal drama you can have with four teens and an infant in the house. Unfortunately, money was very tight, and we struggled because we wanted everything for our kids. I worked non-stop at my new job and even got on the local news and into the local papers, which was awesome for living in a city with 4 million people, like Houston. I did not have the balance I wanted for my life and was running 90 to nothing.

Eight years of marriage passed overnight, and I worked so hard that I got to the point where I could barely walk or hold my bladder, and the doctor said that I would have to have back surgery. Half of our kids were out of the house now. Our daughter Jessica had gotten married and was due to have a baby any day. The salon I worked at was super busy and growing. I was supposed to take the salon over. It had become a half-a-million-dollar business. I was managing marketing and working behind the chair.

I was trying to take care of Michael and be a children's pastor with all that entails. I was basing my whole identity on what I could produce or accomplish. I did not have time to pause and fall apart, but my back was saying something different. If I was going to keep walking, I was going to have to take a break and have back surgery. I kept hoping that it would disappear. I thought it had something to do with my faith or lack thereof. But inevitably, the surgery would be needed.

So, there you have it, a synopsis of my life, up until I died. If I had a dollar for every time someone told me to write a book, I would be rich, rich, rich. My life parodied a soap opera mixed with a Lifetime movie!

TWELVE
KINGDOM CITIZENSHIP

If you have made a decision to follow Christ, you are the family of God. You are a member of a heavenly kingdom realm, which coexists with that of the world. Being a member of God's heavenly kingdom means that you will have rights to that kingdom and responsibilities to that kingdom. The purpose God gives you is unique to you. When you start your journey to discovering God's purpose in your life, there will be a lot of people who have their own idea of how it should happen, if it should happen, or if you even heard from God at all. The people that come forward may surprise you. Do not get angry. Don't worry, pray for them, love them, and focus on your relationship with the Lord. Do not be surprised if it's the people closest to you that doubt the most. People who have known you all your life may not understand God's grace toward you or the direction he is leading you. Trust God! I believe it is simply God's love and grace toward me that He caught me when I needed to be caught and showed me exactly what I needed to see. I was drowning. Then He showed me the world and showed me that so many of them were drowning too. All of us lost in lies that the enemy planted in our lives about who God says we are and how much He loves us. Because of my experience with God, I came back with a God given empathy for people and through the guidance of the Holy Spirit, I proposed to share my story in the hope that what I have learned would speak to someone like me and set them free.

If you have doubts; seek peace.
I've learned to always keep my eyes on God.

> *And if anyone will not receive you or listen to your words, shake off the dust from your feet when you leave that house or town* (Matthew 10:14 ESV).

I met a man once who was a citizen of the United States. He came from Africa. He was a dark-skinned black man with a heavy accent. He worked very hard to learn the language and become an American citizen. One day, he decided to go back to Africa to see his family. When he was in the bathroom of the airport to return to the United States, he left his bag outside the stall. In his bag were his passport, plane tickets, and money. He didn't think he would be but a second, but it only took a second for it to get stolen.

He stood in the airport thinking he was lost. He thought, *who will believe me that I am who I say I am? How will I ever get home to the United States?* An airport clerk saw him and asked him what was wrong, and where did he have his citizenship? When he said he was a United States citizen, the clerk said, "Perfect, go out and hail a cab and go to the US Embassy. The guard there will pay for your cab ride and will bring you into the Embassy. There, they will reestablish your identity and make sure you have back everything that was stolen from you."

The man was shocked, unsure that any of this would happen. He decided he had nothing to lose, so he went out, hailed a cab, and that was exactly what happened. All of his paperwork was restored, and he went on to finish his trip. He saw his family and then came back to the United States almost as if nothing had happened. All because he was a citizen of the United States, and someone knew the laws concerning him.

The consequences without knowing those laws would have been unimaginable.

The same goes for the Kingdom of Heaven. We must know the promises and the scriptures concerning our born-again birthright and cling to them because, without that knowledge we fail to thrive. If you know and love the Lord with all your heart, and your name is written in the Lamb's Book of Life, you are a Kingdom citizen and all the protection and provision that the Kingdom of God has for you is yours.

After all, He is interested in you personally and He is the God of the Universe. Sometimes, we forget who God is. We make Him small like the leader of a country instead of the Creator of the Universe. Remember, the God of the Universe knows your name, He made you for a purpose, and He loves you. If you were the only person on earth, He would have died for you.

When Jesus was asked how to pray, He gave them what is known as the Lord's Prayer. It is the best-known prayer in the Christian world.

> *After this manner, therefore, pray ye: Our Father which art in heaven, Hallowed be thy name. Thy kingdom come, Thy will be done on earth, as it is*

> *in heaven. Give us this day our daily bread. And forgive us our debts, as we forgive our debtors. And lead us not into temptation but deliver us from evil: For thine is the kingdom and the power, and the glory, forever. Amen* (Matthew 6:9-13 KJV).

The words "Thy kingdom come" stand out to me the most because I realize now that the Kingdom of God is an actual government. If I were to go to a foreign country and not know the rules of that government, I could get myself in trouble. If we are to be citizens of the Kingdom of God on earth, then we ought to know the promises of God that apply to us as Christians.

Get to Know Your Father in Heaven

I have to say that when the rubber meets the road and you realize the truth that none of us are promised tomorrow, you need to know who God is to you. You need to know if you have an intimate relationship with Him. Intimacy with God was a hard one for me. I had been molested as a child and had mistaken intimacy as something to distrust, intrusive, and hurtful experience. It was not until I got married to my husband Jim, who is a man of God, that I finally began to learn what a true intimate relationship was. Having an intimate relationship with God is like a marriage. Just like you give yourself in marriage, trusting that person with your life, helping you make decisions, and knowing they have your best interest at heart.

God knows you better than your husband ever will, but do you know God? Just like a marriage, you must trust God with everything in you and about you, your plans, your money, your kids, and your health. You need to know His point of view on things. I was not sure how to do that in the beginning. I knew what I learned in church about God. Now that I had stood in heaven with the Father, I knew what I had done in church was like a chat-line conversation. I needed to really know the Father, Son, and Holy Ghost. I learned that my most intimate times with God are when I worship. It's during times of praise and worship that I often feel the tangible presence of God. It's when I am in the tangible presence of God that many of the questions in my life get answered and I have a peace that surpasses my understanding.

The whole world can be crashing down, and I am at peace because I know no matter what happens, God has my back.

I used to leave church on Sunday and get so busy with my

life that I would not think about Him again until the next time I went to church. After heaven, I realized that going to church was about confirmation that what I had learned from God during the week was true, it was to associate with God's people and to hear their testimonies. It was to build my faith by hearing people talking about the scriptures and understanding how they applied to my life and my situations. There is a lot of church that goes on in my house every day with God. For me, the church has left the building. The word church actually means, "a called-out people." Church is not an event; it is a way of living. The way to know God is to know His Word and acknowledge His nature.

> *In the beginning was the Word, and the Word was with God, and the Word was God. He was with God in the beginning. Through him all things were made; without him, nothing was made that has been made. In him was life, and that life was the light of all mankind. The light shines in the darkness, and the darkness has not overcome it* (John 1:1-5 NIV).

Now that I was starting over and getting to know God, I knew I was going to have to read His Word and study it because it was the beginning of getting to know Him. Not knowing God's Word is like getting married and never having a conversation with your husband. It is not a whole relationship.

Know Who You Are to God

You must know who you are to Christ and where you stand with Him. You need to know that above all things, He loves you. If you have gotten to the place where you are seeking the heart of God and you believe that it is true that He is the only living God and the God of His Word, then this scripture will speak to you about how much He loves you.

> *And I am convinced that nothing can ever separate us from God's love. Neither death nor life, neither angels nor demons, neither our fears for today nor our worries about tomorrow—not even the powers of hell can separate us from God's love. No power in the sky above or in the earth below—indeed, nothing in all creation will ever be able to separate us from the love of God that is revealed in Christ Jesus our Lord* (Romans 8:38-39 ESV).

Understand that God does think about you, you are not just a passing thought; He knows everything about you. You are more than the sum of your highs and lows, the sum of your parts including your looks, your weight, and your degrees. You are a spiritual being made in the image of God, a child of the King of kings, a true heir. The Holy Spirit is ever-present for you, to comfort you, to guide you, and to keep you safe. He picks you up when you have fallen, defends you from the enemy, fights each battle on your behalf, and points you in the right direction. He will give you a new beginning, give back what the enemy has stolen, end your grief, direct you to the right relationships for friendship, encouragement, marriage, and command angels on your behalf. He will even bring you back from the brink of death itself.

God has given His Son to right all the wrongs, heal all the wounds, lift all the judgment to make us whole again, and put us on a good path. He wants great things for you. He will never leave you or forsake you. He has a plan for you, to prosper you. The question is are you going to take the time to know His Word? Are you going to get to know Him well enough that you ask Him, "Lord, I am committing to lay down my life, I am going to give it all, what's the plan?"

> *"For I know the thoughts that I think toward you," says the Lord, "thoughts of peace and not of evil, to give you a future and a hope" (Jeremiah 19:11 NKJV).*

Another translation says, "I know the plans that I have for you, declares the Lord. They are plans for peace and not disaster plans to give you a future filled with hope" (GW).

> *This means that anyone who belongs to Christ has become a new person. The old life is gone; a new life has begun!* (2 Corinthians 5:17 NLT).

Finding your God-led purpose means leaving behind the pain of your past and letting go of all the baggage. It means fearlessly moving forward as if you are convinced that the outcome has already happened. It is also understanding that you may have loved ones and friends that are not ready to go with you because they are not convinced. It's okay to let go and let God work on their hearts and be an example of His love, but you must keep moving forward. People want to be comfortable. You may not always be comfortable but go anyway.

Trust God that He has got you. The good news is that the Gospel says the devil's time is short. You and I are in a battle with many victories and many losses, but death has no victory because we have an eternity with the Lord. The devil's reign is short. We may have collateral damage, but we will endure because we are more than our bodies. We are spiritual beings made in the image of God. We are powerful and strong. The same power that raised Christ from the dead resides in us. We must walk by faith, not by sight as we listen for the still small voice of the Holy Spirit to guide us and lead us.

When I was in the hospital, my purpose was to live. We wrote on the whiteboard in the hospital the greatest purpose scriptures of all time. They are for everyone wherever you are, whatever your position, and whatever your circumstances.

> *Jesus came up and said to them, "All authority (all power of absolute rule) in heaven and on earth has been given to Me. Go therefore and make disciples of all the nations [help people to learn of Me, believe in Me, and obey My words], baptizing them in the name of the Father and of the Son and of the Holy Spirit, teaching them to observe everything I have commanded you; and lo, I am with you always [remaining with you perpetually—regardless of*

> *circumstance, and on every occasion], even to the end of the age"* (Matthew 28:18-20 AMP).

> *I shall not die, but live and declare the works of the Lord* (Psalm 118:17 NKJV).

I had already died and was in the fight for my life. It was important to keep my purpose in front of me day and night.

Focusing on the pain of any kind and especially of the past will grip you, making you rethink decisions that you no longer have control over. That is the wrong focus and will steal precious fleeting moments of your life. It will murder who you could have been. Focus on Christ and His promise in John 10:10 and you will have a life worth living. "The thief does not come except to steal, and to kill and to destroy. [Christ] I have come that they may have life, and they may have it more abundantly" (John 10:10 KJV).

There is a saying that life is too short. This statement is usually about regrets if you get to the end of your life, and you didn't spend it properly. To tell you the truth, life is the moment you are in right now and it's full of opportunities, so what are you going to do with it? You must live in that moment.

Spend your life well, no headstone ever said I loved too much!

Sisterly Advice

Eat Right: I am quite driven and thrive on producing. This gets me in trouble because as my husband always says, "There will always be an inbox, something to do, and work to be done." We have to take time to love and listen to the people around us and be a conduit in the earth for God's love. We also need to take time to love ourselves. I have spent years working hard, not eating right, and not sleeping enough at the expense of my body. I was always at war with my body and convinced that it was carnal and was keeping me from what I wanted to do. The truth is, it is the house of the Holy Spirit and for Him to work properly through us, we need to keep a clean house. The way to do that spiritually and physically is to eat healthy food that is full of nutrients and spiritually to consume the Word of God daily. Jesus said in Mathew 4:4, "It is written, 'Man shall not live by bread alone, but by every word that proceeds from the mouth of God'" (KJV).

Meditate Correctly: We must have time for white space in our minds. Just be quiet for a moment, take time to stop and smell the roses, and meditate. This is a physical thing for a spiritual purpose. It is taking the time to think about things that are good in your life, pure things, and good reports. Philippians 4:8 says, "Finally, brethren, whatever things are true, whatever is noble, whatever things are just, whatever things are pure, whatever things are lovely, whatever things are of good report, if there is any virtue and if there is anything that is praiseworthy meditate on these things" (NKJV).

Rest: Sleep is important. We must take time to rest. It is a time of rejuvenation and an opportunity for godly dreams. It is a time for rebuilding. I spent many nights staying up late making lists on the ceiling in my mind and worrying about all manner of things. It never solved one problem. Rest without anxiety is a faith move, by the way! Psalm 127:2 says, "It is vain for you to rise early, to stay up late, to eat the bread of sorrows (anxiety) for so he gives his beloved sleep" (NKJV).

Praise and Worship with all your heart, soul, and mind: Give praise, adoration, and honor to God from your heart. We usually think of this as singing in church but singing words without a heart of worship makes it unproductive. It is not about me; it's about giving my heart to the Lord with everything in me. It is also a powerful weapon and a reminder to us of who we are, who we belong to, and who our source is. The only thing the devil has is words. If we are worshiping with our whole focus on God, the devil can't act because he has no power over us. Many times, in the Bible the Lord sent out the musicians ahead of the army in battle. Make Psalm 103:1-5 your pattern for worship. "Bless the LORD, O my soul, and all that is within me, bless his holy name! Bless the LORD, O my soul, and forget not all his benefits, who forgives all your iniquity, who heals all your diseases, who redeems your life from the pit, who crowns you with steadfast love and mercy, who satisfies you with good so that your youth is renewed like the eagle's" (ESV).

Pray: To me, prayer is a conversation with God. Talking to God is an artform. I used to only give Him my list of what I needed done. I was like a machine. Now, I try to spend time talking to the Lord and thanking Him for everything He has given me and telling Him how in awe I am of Him. I reflect on my screw-ups and ask for forgiveness. I ask for His help in changing my thought process that got me to that moment in the first place. I try to accept forgiveness and not beat myself up. I thank God for His grace and move on. Then I ask for help and direction. Sometimes, I get answers right away like thoughts that are greater than my capacity. Sometimes, it comes through people and confirmations. Sometimes, it's just wait and see. Sometimes, it is no. Like in a courtroom, I petition the Lord and He gets the ultimate say so.

Don't get me wrong. I make plans and have a calendar. I try to balance everything on that calendar. However, sometimes things happen that I was not expecting. Sometimes, I miss it altogether and nothing turns out how I planned. I always accept that if it didn't happen, God will always use what did. Romans 8:28 says, "We know with great confidence that God, who is deeply concerned about us, causes all things to work together, as a plan, for good for those who love God, to those who are called according to His plan and purpose" (AMP).

I may get delayed or spend extra time talking to a waitress at a restaurant. I may get home and get a phone call asking for advice or prayer and spend an extra hour before I leave the car. I try to walk in God's love for the moment. I try to realize that I am His hands and feet in the earth and if I give my time to God, He multiplies everything back to me.

Work: Work is important. We need to pay bills. God gave Adam a job to work in the garden. God can use you in your work and every part of your life. Not everyone is called to be a pastor or a preacher, but we are called to serve God in all that we do. My suggestion is to work on purpose. You may be a business owner, a bus driver, a housewife, or a corporate CEO. God wants each one of us to work in the gifts He has bestowed on us with excellence. We need to understand our special influence in the world and that we are the reflection of Him in all that we do. Galatians 6:9-10 tells us, "And let us not grow weary of doing good, for in due season we will reap, if we do not give up. So then, as we have opportunity, let us do good to everyone, and especially to those who are of the household of faith" (ESV).

Love: Remember you are a gift for the greater good, not only for the world you influence, but for the people you love. You are beautiful and wonderfully made and unique. You are the only one that can fill your space in the world. You have a unique perspective that is useful if you let it be. God loved you enough to send His only begotten Son for you, to reshape existence so that if you were the only one in the world, He would have had you on His heart.

> *Now, when the Pharisees heard that He had silenced (muzzled) the Sadducees, they gathered together. One of them, a lawyer [an expert in Mosaic Law], asked Jesus a question, to test Him: "Teacher, which is the greatest commandment in*

> *the Law?" And Jesus replied to him, "'You shall love the Lord your God with all your heart, and with all your soul, and with all your mind.' This is the first and greatest commandment. The second is like it, 'You shall love your neighbor as yourself [that is, unselfishly seek the best or higher good for others].' The whole Law and the [writings of the] Prophets depend on these two commandments"* (Mathew 22:34-40 AMP).

Exercise Forgiveness: The pain of the past is only good for the lessons it rendered to spur you to victory today. You must let go of unforgiveness and hurt and choose peace, love, and a sound mind. You must not live on feelings. Forgiveness is a decision, not a feeling. Your feelings will always be unfaithful to you. Cold one minute, hot the next. Forgiveness is a decision you must decide to accomplish. You must die to your physical feelings on the subject and move on. You must take every thought into captivity and control your thought life on the matter. Forgiveness is not the same as tolerance. Forgiveness is concluding that in some way you have been hurt and that it was a device of an unseen enemy. Even though a person has been used for this, you need to give them to God to deal with.

2 Corinthians 10:3 says, "For though we walk in the flesh, we do not war according to the flesh. For the weapons of our warfare are not carnal but mighty in God for pulling down strongholds, casting down arguments and everything that exalts itself against the knowledge of God, bringing every thought into captivity to the obedience of Christ" (NKJV).

I was raped and sexually abused by different people. I had to forgive them. If I focus on my feelings on the matter, I will go back and live in that moment. I choose to live there no more. The enemy used them for that moment and stole it from me, but I will not give them one more moment in my life. However, that does not mean we hang out or that my forgiveness means that they don't have to abide by the laws of the land and suffer the consequences of their sin. I pressed charges and fought back in every way I could at the time. There were times where I could not fight. I beat myself up for what I could or should have done. I give myself grace and I forgive myself for these instances because hindsight is 20/20. I will not think of things that bear me no fruit. I do not live under condemnation any longer. I know who the accuser is, and I can overcome him by the word of my testimony and the blood of the Lamb.

> *Then I heard a loud voice saying in heaven, "Now salvation, and strength and the kingdom of our God, and the power of his Christ have come, for the accuser of our brethren, who accused them before our God day and night, has been cast down. And they overcame [you and I} him by the blood of the lamb and by the word of their testimony, and they did not love their lives to the death* (Revelation 12:10 NKJV).

I have a purpose that is so important in my life that I do not have time to deal with the past situations that the enemy threw at me. I keep my eye on the ball, only relating to it when it has an opportunity to be a testimony for what God brought me out of.

Read God's Word: Knowledge of the Word Is the Weapon of a True Believer. There were times in my life where I might have one promise to hang my hat on, but it was enough. The Bible says very clearly, "My people are destroyed for lack of knowledge" (Hosea 4:6a). However, this is only a partial scripture. God said that we are cursed if we forget the scripture and God from which we have come. There are many consequences so terrible for not knowing and passing on the knowledge of God. This is a chess move we must make. We choose to either know God or to ignore Him. You can't know Him a little or casually or you don't know Him at all.

In Matthew 4:17, Jesus said, "Behold the Kingdom of Heaven is at hand" which means it's here, it's real in the earth and it is a real spiritual realm that you can either choose to walk in or not.

It is your choice. Do bad things happen to good people? Yes, but we win no matter what. That's the Gospel, that's the good news. We transcend the bounds of this world and subscribe to a different set of rules. We are blessed and always favored as citizens of heaven!

Go Fishing: Fishing with Jesus. One night, I came home exhausted and extremely frustrated after street witnessing on Bourbon Street in New Orleans. I went to sleep praying. I had a dream that I was fishing with Jesus. We were sitting on the banks of the Jordan River. I looked to my left, and Jesus was in a white robe with a fishing pole fishing. He looked at me with a big smile and said, "Danielle. I taught you how to fish, but did I ever tell you how I clean the fish?"

"No, Lord," I said.

He immediately brought me over to a table. There, He poured water over the fish, and the first thing He did was take what looked like a square hatchet and cut off the fish's head. This was symbolic of the washing of the Word of God and Jesus having to get past our head so He can begin to change us. Then, He filleted the fish, removing the scales, cutting out the bones, and cleaning out all the inside, the poop, the dirt, the entrails. He came up with a clean pink piece of fish. Those tough outer layers of our life must be cut away and all the junk we keep hidden on the inside must be exposed to Jesus so He can deal with them.

He then took the fish and seasoned it. He begins to give us a new identity, seasoned with godly character, integrity, and love. The next thing He did was throw the fish on the grill. The fish began to crackle and sizzle. Its texture changed, the look of it changed, and a wonderful aroma began to waft from the grill. While still cooking, He began to press down on it. This changed the fish even more from its original state. The struggles we face because we live in a fallen world actually help us change and become stronger and more dependent on Christ. After a few minutes of cooking, He stuck a fork in the fish. He looked at me and smiled at me with a big grin because

He knew that I knew what came next. He said, "Now it's holy and unrecognizable as the body of Christ." Then He put the fish in His mouth, chewed it, and swallowed it, all the while maintaining the happiest joyful smile on His face!

The main two lessons are these. One: although I was sent out to catch fish, it is not my job to clean the fish. It is His! The second is every Christian is in a different phase of their cleaning; that process of becoming what Christ intended them to be. I must show grace to others and to myself and trust what Jesus is doing in our lives. In the end, we are all to become Christ to the world.

Leave a Legacy: My son, Michael said one day, "Mom, what if there are books of the Bible still being written for future generations, and your name was the title of one of those books?"

Wow! What a thought! To think that the book God is writing about me could include the possibility of how God used me to bring a generation to the knowledge of their true birthright, the love of the Father, the privilege, power, and purpose that comes with that. I'm just thankful He knows me and my name is written in His book of life. But we should all live every day as though God is writing our memoir. (In truth, He is!) We shouldn't live this way for our own kudos, but for others to see the goodness of our wonderful, loving Father!

Start by reviewing this list of what God has taught me so you can take full advantage of life's opportunities and serve Him and others. Check off the ones you need to work on in your own life. Then go back and review what I shared in this chapter about them. Practice balance in your life.

- ✓ Eat Right
- ✓ Meditate Correctly
- ✓ Rest
- ✓ Praise and Worship with all your heart, soul, and mind
- ✓ Pray
- ✓ Work
- ✓ Love
- ✓ Exercise Forgiveness
- ✓ Go Fishing
- ✓ Leave a Legacy

The way to know God is to know His Word and acknowledge His nature. You must know who you are to Christ and where you stand with Him. So, are you going to take the time to know His Word?

Are you going to get to know Him well enough that you ask Him, "Lord, I am committing to lay down my life, I am going to give it all, what's the plan?"

THIRTEEN
WRITING THIS BOOK AND OVERCOMING FEAR

"And who knows but that you have come to your royal position for such a time as this?" (Esther 4:14b NIV)

Testing the Water

I didn't come back after dying and spending nearly six months in the hospital with the idea of sharing my story with the world. In the beginning, I worried what people might think, and I only told my story to a few people. I was testing the water, getting a feeling for what people's reactions would be to my experience. I was surprised at the range of reactions. The reactions seemed to fall into categories. Some people were emotionally moved and connected in a new way with God. My story seemed to validate what they hoped was true. Some people I met just didn't believe me. They seemed to think that I was a little crazy. But, since the love of God that I experienced had affected me so powerfully, I risked scrutiny and continued to share my story. People need to know that God loves them individually and is particularly interested in their lives. The reaction that perplexed me the most was people who were dismissive. To my surprise, most of them were believers in Christ. My expectation was that they of all people would be excited and emotionally moved at the confirmation that heaven was real. However, quite a lot of them seemed complacent. It was almost as if they had heard it before; that this was simply another Sunday school story, which they had heard a million times. My hope was that people would lean in, get excited, and want questions answered about God.

I suppose if the tables were turned and I was certain I believed in God, I might have been afraid to ask questions myself about what Heaven would really be like, thinking it was like questioning my faith. I now know that before my experience, I had many questions that were unanswered, like

"Doubting Thomas" in the Bible, who needed to touch Jesus to believe he was real. When I would come across people like this, in my mind I would think, "Hold on, wait a minute, you didn't hear me. I met **The Creator of the universe**; don't you want to know what happened?"

I decided to give it to God and let Him decide. I simply would pray and ask God if I were supposed to share my story with people that I would encounter. If He answered yes, I would do it and if He said no, I would not and move on. So, let this be an encouragement to those of you who have something to share with the world about God. Remember, not everyone is ready to hear what you have to say. Sometimes, God is preparing their hearts to receive. Even if you do not get the response you hoped for, you are planting a seed.

Whatever the reaction to my story may be, my prayer is that people are changed and that the reality of what I shared will forever change how they see themselves and deepen their relationship with God.

I love talking about God's astonishing love! The profound feeling of peace and indescribable joy I experienced in heaven comes flooding back every time I share my story.

I Almost Rushed Because of My Addiction

I wanted so badly for other people to understand the revelation of what I had experienced; I was over-eager to share what I knew in spite of many unanswered questions. I knew I did not have all the pieces to the puzzle. God was working on me and showing me my faulty motivation. If I had written the book without the answers to the questions, I would still be lost today. Deep inside I knew I needed to savor what God was teaching me. I almost did what I had always done. I always sought instant approval from people mistaking it for unconditional love. I always sought unconditional love from people! I looked for what only God could give me from people. I had an approval addiction. I lived under the lie that I could make someone love me. However, I came back with so much unconditional love from heaven, I realized I had to tell my whole story the good, the bad, and the ugly and that it would not have the impact it should if I were not totally real with you. There are things about my life that I had to write that were a struggle to write. So, I have to say that it took nothing less than putting my whole heart, mind, body, and spirit into this book, to convey just a small part of what an impact this experience had on me.

Why Me, Processing What God had Called Me to Do

I started to search the scriptures, pray, and ask God to help me write this book. It has not been as easy a road as I thought it would be to map out this experience. Everything changed in my mind which in turn changed my life.

> *Search me, O God, and know my heart! Try me and know my thoughts! And see if there be any grievous way in me and lead me in the way everlasting!* (Psalm 139:23-24 ESV).

God shared His unique love with me personally, and then showed me His intense love for you. In writing this book, I spent a lot of time going back over the past trauma in my life and reliving the pain. For the first time in my life, I began to recognize the lies that drove me and recognized that Satan, through these lies, had enslaved me. This process of reexamining my life was extremely difficult and painful, but necessary. Sometimes, we must know the truth of where we have come from and unravel the lies to enjoy the blessing of the inheritance of our true God-given identity and to be set free.

Although I had always seen myself as a list of labels:

Mom, wife, professional, fat, tired, sad, happy, loved, unloved, married, unmarried, pretty, ugly, smart, stupid, rich, or poor. I now know that I was much more than the sum of my labels, my appearance or my accomplishments or even the bad things that had happened to me. I knew after my journey to heaven, that the purpose God planted in me long before I was ever placed on this earth was bigger than me and what He had intended for my life was more important than any jobs I could hold, awards I could win, or the number that was in my bank account and even my personal appearance.

I believe that life needs God's spark to mean anything. I know this because when I thought I was dying the only regrets I had were the ones that had to do with loving people. We need to know that we are building an eternal legacy. I did not want to think about anything in my past after I died. I wanted to bask in the glory of my new revelation and forget the past altogether. However, I knew that my story would never be as impactful as it could be for the Kingdom of God if I did not bare my soul and take you on the journey with me and show you what God showed me.

As I wrestled with God about going over the past, I realized God had given His Son Jesus for us, so I knew following his example, that I should not hold back. I should let you in on all the stuff I wanted to forget, along with the lessons I learned, in hopes that if you identified, you could understand the true healing that came out of my new relationship with God. As it should be in your journey that God puts you on, strive to give your best!

What the Lord put on my heart to do is to help others follow God's purpose for their lives by documenting my lessons through the filter of heaven.

The Struggle Is Real, But You Will Overcome

I will warn you, when you start on the process of figuring out who you are, what you are meant to do in life, and realizing your purpose in this world, there will be naysayers. These are people who either can't see your vision or who believe they are saving you from the pain of failure. Remember, failure is just a lesson on how to do it better. Intentions are good, but remember you must stand before the Lord alone. If God tells you to do it, even if you are only 75% sure and think you might look foolish or fail, my advice to you is to do it anyway.

I came across some opposition from places I never expected from people I deeply respected. I came back from heaven so full of revelation, believing that the world would want to hear what

I learned. However, some of the people I loved and respected did not think they wanted me to write my story. Sometimes, people fear guilt by association. They are afraid of what people will think of them. However, each person that did not want me to tell my story taught me another lesson about who I was and who God called me to be.

Each person is around you for a reason. Make it a positive one. I began to realize that people play a large role in our lives, especially the people we respect. My only desire is to please one person, Jesus Christ. The critics are always looking for something to criticize no matter how good your intentions. So, when you go after your dreams, remember those people are a fixture and no matter what you do, they will always be there with their opinion. Listen but don't act until you pray about it and seek the guidance of the Holy Spirit. Keep going and stay focused on your God-given identity and your God-driven purpose.

Send Baby Moses Down the River

I remember talking to my publishing coach, Peter Lopez, and asking, "Peter, am I ready to send this book to edit, are you sure I am ready?"

In my mind, I thought, "This is important! This is one of

the most important things I've ever done in my life." I knew I would stand before the Lord with this. I try to remember when I do something now, to do it for the glory of the Lord, for He is our only hope.

Peter quietly listened to me tell my story, paused, and said, "Man, you are for real!"

I was so passionate about the phone call, so emotional, I could hear in his voice that he was mindfully listening to me. Peter has been an author, writer, and preacher for a long time. He is now encouraging others who write books. I suppose you could say that Peter's purpose is to help others launch their God-inspired words.

He answered my plea, with this, "Danielle that book is your Moses. You need to put baby Moses in the basket and send him down the river to God so he can fulfill his purpose and grow up and come back and free the slaves."

I never forgot that!

I identified with being a slave. I had been a slave to my feelings of unworthiness since I was a small child. I had a family that loved me, but I had the experience of being abused, neglected, let down, assaulted, and disappointed. I had come through it all with Jesus Christ. There seemed to be one hardship or tragedy after another with a great deal of teachable moments in between. God would pull me up and out of every situation. I was a walking testimony. I believed that this was the will of God for me. I had major scars, reminders, aches, and pains leftover from the battle, so I embraced the idea of being superwoman, believing the lie that it would make me worthy to be loved.

I became a lot like the Genie in the Aladdin story. I would pop up and say, "What do you need, what do you want? What can I do for you?" I got all my self-worth from people. I was a slave to what people thought and worst of all, what I thought of myself and the lies the enemy had fed me all my life. I knew Jesus was awesome. However, there were painful things about myself I did not hand over to God. My mantra was "I will fake it till I make it," which meant I was a fake. I hid painful things about myself. I turned the attention away from my brokenness by trying to be a people pleaser, and an overachiever, pushing myself to my breaking point at whatever I could do. I got great satisfaction out of trying to fix everything in any person's life who would let me.

I became like a porcupine. I would be neck deep in your business, but no one could get close to me. It was always going to be about the other person. When I wasn't doing that, I was deep in the trenches, solving my own terrible problems that read something like a television soap opera.

I could write a whole dramatic book about my life. Some of you might think I have, but what I want you to take away is how far I had come in my thinking to write this book. In the beginning, I could only list what happened to me. To tell you the story has meant feeling every painful moment and reliving painful memories all over again. But with God, I did it!

FOURTEEN
I FOUND MYSELF IN HEAVEN!

Over the years, I would pray with people and tell them my story. Each person would ask me questions about heaven, God, salvation, and destiny. Every time I would tell my story, there would be a moment I could see in their eyes that there was a piece in it for them. There was something that happened in my life or some revelation I was given that could change their perspective of God and their identity through Christ.

One day, I was praying with a girl. It had been three years since my heaven experience. She was telling me about her low self-worth. She did not like some things about herself. These handicaps she had physically, or that she perceived that she had, caused her not to believe that she was beautiful or important or special in any way. She kept looking for a formula, a way to perfect herself, change her outward appearance, improve her health, or increase her knowledge.

When I first met her, she had been overweight and extremely unhealthy. She was a literal basket case. I knew on the day I met her that there was nothing I could sell her from my salon that was going to fix her. I put her on the path of seeing several doctors that could help her health needs and prayed with her that day for salvation to renew her life with the Lord as she was already a believer.

Over the years, I saw her transformation. She overcame cancer, lost 70 pounds, her hair grew back, and she changed everything about her regimen health-wise. I was in awe of her transformation. Yet, she could not see it. She had accomplished so many of the things that I was struggling to accomplish. For both of us, perfection on this earth was unattainable.

She came in one day for a haircut, which I knew meant prayer. I encouraged her and pointed out all her accomplishments. She encouraged me and gave me credit for the advice. Yet, with all she had accomplished, she was still unhappy. Her walk with the Lord was closer than it had ever been, but she still felt like a failure.

Who was I to give any advice? I had been to Heaven and back and had not accomplished half as much. So, we started to pray, and the Lord had a word. It was for her, it was for me, and it is for you.

The Lord told me to get real for her. I pointed out to her that I am still overweight. That I have things in my body that are not completely healed yet. That we all put on airs to be something we are not.

I said, "These are just tent clothes. I am a spiritual being that owns a body. I am the temple of the Holy Spirit. It is up to me to stay strong and govern my body, but I am more than the sum of the hairs on my head or anything that defines the physical being. I must wake up every morning and look in the mirror and remind myself that I AM that woman the Lord showed me in Heaven. I am constantly working with the Lord to pull out the weeds in my life."

Inspired by a revelation from the Holy Spirit, I said to her, "Even when I was in Heaven, the Lord showed me a long line of people who I could impart God's love to and introduce them to the little piece of Heaven that I found."

Then, I told her that the fact she was sitting in front of me, through whatever circumstances, meant that she was on the mind and in the heart of God, and He loved her desperately.

I asked her, "Don't you understand? I am that woman! The one I saw in heaven and everything that she encompasses. You are that woman too! So, every day, when you wake up and the enemy yells at you and says 'Look at how imperfect you are! Look how unworthy you are! Look at all your lack! Look at the mistakes you've made! Does God really love you?' Tell him to shut up! There will always seem to be obstacles There will always be things to get in the way. It's when we come to the end of ourselves and we start to walk in the Spirit and begin each day with eternity in mind, that we begin to overcome the devices of the enemy."

She asked, "What was the formula?"

I answered, "There is no formula. There is an intimate relationship with God which puts Him in charge of our daily decisions and opens opportunities to love people into the Kingdom of Heaven, into the knowledge of their true birthright, and to embrace the promises from the Word of God which belong to them. There is nothing else more important than loving people with the love of God right where we are at. If you are somewhere you don't want to be, use it as an opportunity, because someone else is there, too."

I realized that all the testimonies and the battles I had fought and been through were no longer for my benefit, but hers. Each one of us can sharpen each other by sharing our testimonies, our mistakes, and our victories. After all, the bible says that iron sharpens iron. Everything I went through was being used as a benefit for her and for you. God uses everything. God has you on His mind. Since you are reading this book, you are part of the group I saw in heaven. If there is only one message you take with you, God loves you. You are the one who God loves, cares for, thinks about, and the one who He desires a relationship with.

God gave me a choice. I had to go to heaven to realize the choice that I was given. You don't have to go to heaven and back. The choice is yours right now. You do not have to be perfect or spiritual. The Kingdom of Heaven is already here. It is up to you to pick up your sword, put on the full armor of God, and go to the front line. Trust me, you do not have to be a television evangelist or anyone famous. You can change lives through the love of God in your sphere of influence. God can use you and your talents exactly the way you are right now.

You are God's masterpiece. With all the beauty in the world, He chose to make you. All you need to do is be a willing vessel and listen to what God says to do. Then step out in faith and do it. All of Heaven will back you up, all the way.

If there is a formula I would say, know your enemies. One of them is Satan and everything that goes with that. The other is in your mind. You have heard the phrase, "garbage in, garbage out." With us as followers of Jesus Christ, the phrase is "God's Word in, God's Word out!" So, put God's Word in you every day. The Word of the Lord does not return void. He cannot lie. It is up to you to take the leap of faith, allow hope to rise, believe God, and allow Him to move the mountains in your life. God cannot work beyond your free will or your unbelief, but if you believe His promises, He can work miracles in your life.

And always remember...

You are who God says you are. You are beautiful, wonderfully made, a magnificent creation, worthy of love, powerful in Him, and a force to be reckoned with for the Kingdom of Heaven! Remind yourself every day, **I Am That Person**! **The one God says I am**. When you look in the mirror, smile back. You are known, you are loved, you are thought about, and God wants to be in your life. He is rooting for you to win!

Prayer

If you have never accepted God's gift of forgiveness and eternal life, please pray the prayer below today. Do not wait any longer to receive His loving gift. Then share with your family, friends, and everyone you meet the truth that you have discovered.

> *Dear Heavenly Father, thank You for Your love. Thank You for revealing to me what Your Son Jesus has done to give me the opportunity to ask for and receive Your forgiveness for my sins. I accept Your gift and ask You to fill me with Your Holy Spirit so that I can move forward and fulfill the destiny and purpose You have for my life. I love You, Father. I look forward to spending eternity with You. In Jesus' name I pray.*

Include this in your journal and make a list of those you want to share your decision with. Diligently study your Bible and find some strong Christians to help you grow in wisdom as you read His Word. Ask God to reveal to you that which you don't understand. He enjoys having His children come to Him for advice and answers. He is a loving Father who wants you not only to prosper but to live a full and fulfilling life with Him here on earth and eventually in heaven. Go ahead and ask Him to refine and define all that is you in his eyes!

Be sure to go to www.IFoundMyselfInHeaven.com and sign the RSVP list for the gate party in heaven!

NOTES

Chapter 3

Special thanks to Lauri Mauldin who provided me with Essential Oils which led people to my hospital room and ultimately to salvation. Lauri can be reached at Lauri.Mauldin@gmail.com.

Chapter 13

Peter Lopez, Publishing Coach and CEO of Publify Press

www.PublifyPress.com

Made in the USA
Coppell, TX
19 January 2022